Duane Harden

5 EASY STEPS to FINANCIAL FREEDOM

DO WHAT YOU LOVE & GET RICH DOING IT

CEOeBooks

An Imprint of Harden Press, New York

5 EASY STEPS

90-Day Action Plan

The Blueprint

Finding Your "I" in Passion

Cleaning Up The Clutter

Say Yes

CEOeBooks

An Imprint of Harden Press,
a Division of ROCEDU Equities, LLC

P.O. Box 1835
New York, New York 10026-2551

LCCN: 2011960377
ISBN-13: 978-0-9848227-0-6
IBSN-10: 0-9848227-0-4

Business & Economics/Entrepreneurship
For information about special discounts for bulk purchases,
Please contact CEOeBooks at orders@ceoebooks.com.

Made in the USA, Charleston, SC

Read & Give

The author of this book participates in our "*Read & Give*" program. As part of our company's legacy, a portion of the profits from every book sold is donated to charity. We thank you for purchasing this book and allowing it to make a difference in your life and the World around you. If you have a charity you would like for our community to support, please visit http://www.hardenpress.com for more information.

Dedication

To the entrepreneurs who will read this
book and create opportunities where others
find despair

Contents

———●———

Acknowledgements

---●---

I must first acknowledge God. I have grown to understand and to appreciate my belief that, without my Creator's guidance, I would not have had the strength to make it through my life's challenges. And I must say that I have seen some truly difficult days and have overcome many trials and tribulations during my investing endeavors. And guess what? They're not over. More problems are sure to come with each new investment I make, and, even with the current ones I have, problems develop as I continue to expand my holdings. But, hey, challenges are what make the game of life interesting. Each and every day, I become older, wiser, and stronger, so bring it on, Universe—I'm ready to handle whatever you throw my way.

I must acknowledge the work of Robert Kiyosaki, whose teachings inspired me to become the powerful force I am today. I must acknowledge my mom. She is the cornerstone of my team's success. Without her patience and unyielding strength, the team would not exist.

Thanks to my cousin Maurice for recommending that I read Kiyosaki's Rich Dad, Poor Dad: What the Rich Teach Their Kids about Money—That the Poor and Middle Class Do Not! Your phone call from Japan changed my life. Next to the Bible, it's the best book I've ever read, and I hope that this book makes as much of a difference in other people's lives as Kiyosaki's did in mine.

And finally, I must apologize to the world, as it has taken me three years to finally do something concrete with my growing inspiration. My newfound love is helping others become the people they are truly destined to be. My goal for you is to achieve financial freedom through reading this book. I have kept this knowledge to myself for too long and showed up late to the party, but at least I'm here now, so come join me! If you read this book and authentically complete the Life Assignments and the Action Plans, I guarantee success is on your horizon.

Introduction

"Nobody can go back and start a new beginning, but anyone can start today and make a new ending."
—Maria Robinson

Chapter 1

Empowering People with Financial Freedom

You are empowered with financial freedom in all areas of your life.

It is so important to set the stage for what you and I are about to do. Chances are we have never met in person, yet you are trusting me to empower you. How do I know this? You purchased this book because of your burning desire to *Do What You Love & Get Rich Doing It*. Starting right now, you are rewriting your history and creating your future, and I admire you for your trust, courage, unyielding commitment, and generosity. In fact, say these words out loud: "I am empowered with financial freedom in all areas of my life." Didn't that feel fantastic? In fact, it felt so good that I want you to repeat this phrase at least ten more times before reading any further.

Did your voice get louder as you were unleashing your empowerment, or did your voice and your enthusiasm fade with each repetition? Think back to when you were a kid and remember all the fun you had playing games. Some games you played alone, some games you played with others, some games you absolutely hated, some games were just okay, and some games you absolutely loved and couldn't wait to play them again. Well, life itself is a game, the biggest you will ever play. The problem is that you have forgotten how much fun you used to have playing games when you were a kid, or perhaps the game of life you're playing right now just isn't fun. As you read, these concepts will become clear to you. The game that you were playing is over, and it is time to create a new game. This time, you are playing with a different set of rules, which you get to make up yourself. This book will help you play the financial freedom game, teaching you how to win at it and how to love playing so much that you would rather do nothing else in life than keep on playing. Now let's have some fun . . . ready . . . set . . . go!

Chapter 2

Who is Duane Harden?

My name is Duane Harden. I'm an ordinary man doing extraordinary things. It has been a lifelong process, but I've finally discovered that what I'm really passionate about is empowering others to become the people they are destined to be. I love people so much that I refuse to quit helping them. In fact, this is the second version of this book I've written, but this time I'm taking a totally different approach to make it even more useful for you. So let's have fun discovering who you really are!

I was working at UPS when I read Kiyosaki's book, *Rich Dad, Poor Dad*. I was inspired, but wasn't fully clear on how to move forward. Through work with contacts and mentors, together with my own determination, I was able to move into the music industry and buy my first cash-flow generating property. Eventually, in a few years, I owned over twenty properties, and banks were turning me down for loans. I went to work for Washington Mutual in order to learn how to structure loan deals for investors like myself and to build my Rolodex. I was the top employee in loans closed in their Harlem office until they closed in 2008.

My desire to share my passion for investment real-estate with others led me to start and lead a cash-flow club in the Harlem section of New York City. Through word of mouth, it grew from six to over six hundred members who help each another to achieve their goals of financial freedom. Countless people have been able to resign from their day job and make money doing something that they love.

In addition to my work with real-estate, I continue to be involved with the music industry, a grocery store, the restaurant business with a healthy food quick service franchise on the Upper West Side of Manhattan and most recently the publishing business. I love to have fun while investing, and I find that this variety helps keep things exciting for me.

Are you ready for my view on prolific wealth? It's plentiful, with more than enough wealth to go around. The Creator has blessed people with everything they could ever possibly want and need in life. The difference between who I am today and who I was ten years ago is that I've had an epiphany as a result of my investing: people have been supplied with an overabundance of wealth, but the key to success is recognizing that it's there to be used. I've also noticed that, to become even more successful, once I've used a resource, I must give something back to the universe so someone else might enjoy its abundance as well: "Give and it shall be given unto you" (Luke 6:38).

The decisions that I made along the way changed my life, and I want to share what I learned with you.

Chapter 3

Why You Should Read This Book

You were browsing through an online store, or perusing the shelves of a bookstore. You heard an advertisement somewhere, or a friend told you about it. Something has led you to this book. I've told you what you can expect, but you're not sure how this book is going to transform your life. I don't blame you. I was a skeptic of books like this myself, so I know all of the emotions you're experiencing right now. You know you want to make financial changes in your life but you don't know how to go about it.

Did you know that your brain's mental capacity is the size of the earth and you are currently only using one-thousandth of it? You have the knowledge but may not know how to organize it, store it, retrieve it, and use it to accomplish your goals. In the film *Limitless* (2011), Eddie Morra, the main character played by Bradley Cooper, is an aspiring writer suffering from writer's block. All looks grim, as he has a looming deadline for a book for which he's already accepted advance payment. As fate would have it, he runs into his ex-wife's brother, who tells Eddie that he has this amazing new drug called NZT that would allow Eddie to tap into his full potential. Eddie takes the pill and is suddenly transformed into his heightened self, reaching unlimited potential. Eddie finishes the book in record speed. This book is the pill that will allow you to unlock your unlimited financial potential.

In this book, you will go through easy step-by-step instructions on how to clear up the clutter in your life, identify your passion, and transform it into a moneymaking business. This book is all about action, and not about theory. By the time you finish reading this book and working through its exercises, you will have put your plan into motion and will already be on your way to owning the business or businesses that will lead you to financial freedom.

EASY STEP

Simply Say Yes!

"Never allow a person to tell you no who doesn't have the power to say yes."

—*Eleanor Roosevelt*

Chapter 4

Just Say Yes

It's harder to say *no* then it is to say *yes*. The moment you say *no*, you instantly close the door to any opportunities that were present. Your life immediately takes a completely different course as a result of that *no* than it would have following a *yes*. Imagine living a "what **is**" life as opposed to a "what **could have been**" life. Living life fully means living with no regrets, taking action and not judging those choices as "right" or "wrong."

People have a tendency to make life harder than it really is, thus disabling themselves from taking action. It's rather easy, if you think about it. Taking action merely means just taking a step; in this situation, it's a step toward being empowered with financial freedom in all areas of your life. Let's look at where the Power of No comes from. Acknowledging its root source will uncover the root source for the Power of Yes.

The term "financial freedom" has many different definitions, and some are certainly complex, but this book keeps it simple by using

Kiyosaki's definition: financial freedom is that mathematical point in the equation where the sum of your passive income exceeds the sum of your expenses. Some tools later in the book will help you define this point in your life. But for now, let's just say that the term means you have the money to do what you want to do when you want to do it.

Have you ever heard the saying "time is money?" You have two precious resources at your disposal: time and money. You can create money, but you can't create time; thus, time is your most precious resource. Think of all the things you do now with your time. How do you spend most of your day? Do you spend it at work? Family activities? Watching TV? Playing video games? Surfing the Web? Now think about the things you spend your money on. Do you spend most of your money on living expenses? Clothes? Entertainment? Vacation and travel? You're probably like most people I meet who say they never have enough time or money to do what they want to do. Hindsight is twenty-twenty, but consider all the missed opportunities that could have reshaped your present-day financial circumstances. This book deals with the reasons that prevented you from taking action, because not taking action at all is the same as saying *no*.

I've been leading a cash-flow club, based in large part on Kiyosaki's principles, in Harlem since November 2003. What puzzles me the most as leader of this group is that from the very first day they join, some members say *yes*, immediately absorb the necessary information, put it into practice, and start walking the path towards financial freedom. Some members who have been in the group since its inception *still* haven't chosen to say *yes*. And some members didn't say *yes* to life until they had been laid off during this last recession.

The movie *Extraordinary Measures* (2010) stars Brendan Fraser as John Crowley and Harrison Ford as research scientist Robert Stonehill. John and his wife, Aileen (played by Keri Russell), form a biotechnology company to develop a drug to save the lives of their two dying children, ages eight and six, who have a life-threatening disease. The parents are faced with many challenges, but they let nothing stop them from raising money to fund Dr. Stonehill's research on Pompe disease. They are triumphant and save their children's lives. What inspired me the most about this movie is that it's based on a true story adapted from Geeta Anand's book *The Cure: How a Father Raised $100 Million—and Bucked the Medical Establishment—in a Quest to Save His Children.*

Why does it take extraordinary measures for some human beings to rise to greatness and to live life in the Power of Yes? John Crowley had so many opportunities to say *no* and to give up, but he knew that taking no action was not an option in his life. He knew that he must do everything in his power to help find a cure for Pompe disease, because his kids' lives depended on it. Will it take something equally traumatic for you to finally say yes to life?

Taking action is a brave act that requires courage, commitment, and drive. Another depiction of the Power of Yes is the portrayal of Chris Gardner's life in the movie *The Pursuit of Happyness*. Will Smith portrays a heroic man who, while raising his young son, rises from homelessness to become an entrepreneur, stockbroker, motivational speaker, and philanthropist. A *no* is a *yes* in the waiting room, and because it takes more work to say *no*, learn to say yes to opportunities and possibilities as they appear in life. John Crowley and Chris Gardner had ample opportunities to say *no*, but they chose to say *yes*. Stop losing money and killing time. Simply say *yes*.

EASY
STEP

•

Cleaning Up
The Clutter

*"The greatest revolution of our generation is the discovery
that human beings, by changing the inner attitudes of their
minds, can change the outer aspects of their lives."*

—*William James*

Chapter 5

Be Careful Whom You Listen To

I have paid upwards of $20,000 to attend one seminar, only to find out later that I was listening to a bonehead. The information he was giving out in his three-day course was nothing I didn't already know; additionally, some of the information was misleading and even downright inaccurate. I've since learned that you have to be careful whom you listen to. Do your homework on the people who are advising you. Find out whether they have successfully accomplished the goals you're trying to achieve. Otherwise, you'll just have another bonehead giving you useless information or something you could have read in a book. To reassure you, here's a little bit more background information on me.

Like any other single parent, my mother unselfishly gave her all while raising two boys alone. She was declared physically disabled from a car accident when I was young. She deserves a Nobel Prize for her amazing feat in keeping our household afloat on just disability income and monthly child support from my dad. However, being raised without a silver spoon in my mouth as a result of my mother's misfortune was a blessing in disguise for me. The Creator does not make mistakes, and although it may seem unclear in any present moment, a divine plan is always in play. I honestly believe that if my childhood had not included the adversity I experienced, I wouldn't have grown to appreciate and to respect the life, happiness, and wealth that I have today.

At an early age, I knew that I had very little desire to work. It was as if I developed some allergic reaction to the mundane concept of being employed. Life had to offer more than just the destiny of higher education, about forty years of mindless and unfulfilling labor, and eventual retirement in sunny Florida. The only potential silver lining was that I would have the love and support of my family and friends as I progressed through life. Determined not to be resigned to this path in life, I vowed to rewrite this unwritten rule. I began to forge my own plan at an early age. I recognized that I wanted something different, so in the eighth grade I committed to two great goals: to become a computer engineer and to retire by age thirty-five. Was that declaration a stroke of pure genius, simply a sign of clear laziness, or a result of a brief state of delirium? How many eighth graders have already figured out that working is for the birds? I don't know when in my childhood I developed this severe allergy to working, but I'm certainly glad I did. And, even so, my mother made sure that I wasn't completely lazy, as I certainly had my share of chores to do around the house. But still, my goal of not working another day past age thirty-five has been my daily quest since the moment I declared it.

My first goal was to become a computer engineer. While

growing up, I realized you had to do more than just play the game—you had to hold the right cards. Unlike the majority of what seemed to be small-minded and rather depressing people around me, I knew that if I played this game of life using the poverty card, the race card, the "give me" card, or any other victim "card," this negative way of thinking would leave me unsuccessful, miserable, and only half alive. Most opportunities do not exist until you create them. If you're sitting around waiting for something to happen, I hate to disappoint you, but it won't. Super humans do not exist. Everyone was created equally, with locked and unlocked potential and the free will to make choices. *No* situation exists in which you do not have a choice. Regardless of how bad your situation may appear to be, you have the choice to let the outcome affect you in a positive or a negative way. Successful people have simply made the choice to be successful, and no person or event can dissuade them from this goal.

I visited my high school guidance counselor one day to discuss the direction of my college plans. I made it quite clear that I wanted to study Computer Engineering. My institutions of choice were Georgia Tech, MIT, and Boston University. The counselor responded that I had neither the aptitude nor family finances to attend any of these schools. At the time, I thought her advice was the worst thing that someone in her position could have said, but I'm now glad she did. Her negativity impacted me so much that I just knew I had to prove her wrong. When I get my mind set on doing something, I cannot be stopped. In this situation, I chose success as the path to take in life as opposed to the course she tried to chart for me. My ship was going to sail in a different direction.

I set out on my mission to get accepted not into just any college but into one of my three top choices. I was far from upset by the counselor's advice, but I was definitely on a quest to be proven right—to prove not to my counselor or to the world but to *myself* that I was destined for success. I went to the public library and checked out a couple of books on college admissions. I researched the requirements for my schools of choice and found they were all about the same. The first requirement I was deficient in was one year of Physics credit. Again, choices…what should I do? Should I harness the Power of No or the Power of Yes? Because I hadn't studied physics yet, I could choose to let my dream end there or find a solution to continue on my path toward greatness. I had the pleasure of attending what I considered then to be an average high school in Savannah. I wasn't privileged enough to live on the "right side of tracks," where the taxpayers' dollars bolstered the better-quality public schools, and my mom certainly didn't have the money to send me to a private school. However, I was determined to get into one of my schools of choice. I requested a meeting with my high school principal to voice my concerns about getting accepted into college and how I refused to let a small requirement like one year of Physics stop me, so I wanted to know what I could do to take the class. It wasn't easy by any means. My heart was racing with fear of rejection, fear of failure, and fear of anything else my mind could think of—those ideas just flowed through my mind nonstop at amazing speed. Just think, I was requesting the administrator of an already-strapped school budget to reallocate resources to add another discipline to the school's curriculum, seeking to make a difference not only in my life but in the lives of all the other students who would follow. Yet I learned a life lesson that day, as the principal told me that if I would circulate a petition and get at least twenty-five students to sign up for a Physics class, he would do his part to find a qualified teacher. My perspiration stopped, as I was pretty popular among my peers and felt confident that I could convince them to do almost anything. However, asking them to add more work to their already-heavy course loads might have been pushing my luck. I don't know how I did it, but I was able to convince more than enough of my peers to sign the petition. To this day, my alma mater still offers Physics as part of its curriculum.

The next college admissions requirement was computer experience, yet another obstacle in my path. It only made sense that if I were to have a strong application to present to the admissions department, I needed computer courses on my transcript. Given that my high school didn't have a Physics course, you can imagine the (nonexistent) status of its computer-course curriculum.

When I made my eighth-grade declaration to become a computer engineer, I certainly didn't wait until high school to start preparing. I used to always beg my mom to take me to Kmart and other discount department stores to buy books on computer programming. While other kids were outside playing ball, I would sit for hours reading those books and writing little BASIC language applications. What's rather hilarious is that we didn't even own a computer, so I had no way to test my program code. I would sit and run each line of code through my head to see whether I would get the expected results. Computers operate on pure logic, yet there was nothing logical about what I was doing. But pretending that I was a computer certainly made me happy. I'd rather do nothing else on a sunny summer day. This activity went on for quite some time. After I did some hard praying and heavy persuading, my father finally brought me a computer. When I opened that box one early Christmas morning to discover I was the proud owner of a brand new Tandy TRS-80 Color Computer, you would have thought I'd won the lottery—and in my eyes, I had. The world was now filled with endless possibilities. I had been like a painter without a canvas. I couldn't wait to finally run all the programs I had written down on paper and spent hours discovering whether they really worked as I had predicted. I had found my first love.

As much as I loved my new TRS-80, it didn't change the fact that I was still missing the required computer credits on my high school transcript. I needed to find another way to strengthen my application. My plate was already full—if I could have created twenty-five hour days in an eight-day week, I certainly would have. My already-exhausting schedule included attending high school classes during the day and working thirty-two hours per week as a hotel front-desk clerk, but I had to find a way to stretch it a little further. With my mom's permission, at age sixteen I enrolled in computer-programming classes at Savannah Vo-Tech. I was the youngest student in my professor's night class. Oh, and at age seventeen, I convinced my mom to grant permission for yet another activity: joining the U.S. Naval Reserves. So after attending military boot camp in my summer between my junior and senior year, I now had one weekend per month that belonged to Uncle Sam to fulfill my military obligation. I needed the GI Bill tuition assistance and my reserve weekend pay to help me through college. Although it was rather tiresome trying to maintain some form of social life, attending two schools, and working, I was still able to graduate from high school and night school with honors. I'm not Superman, but boy did I try to come close to being him. In retrospect, I think many people lived childhoods very similar to mine—everyone has experienced adversities that required superhuman powers to overcome. And life always presents more adversities, against which people muster up those same powers to prevail.

A small excerpt from my future heart-warming autobiography made it into the pages of my college-admissions application essay. I wasn't trying to create a tearjerker or to reach out for sympathy, as there is no room for sympathy in the pure facts of life. Many other people have truly walked a much more difficult path than I. But nevertheless, my essay touched one admissions director so much that he flew down from MIT just to meet me. Finally, I decided to attend Boston University, the seventh most expensive university in the country at that time. Working my way through college wasn't easy, but when the dean of BU's College of Engineering called my name to walk across the stage to receive my BS degree in Computer Engineering, it was music to my ears and joy to my soul. I had accomplished half of my eighth-grade plan for success.

I can't overemphasize how important it is to realize that everyone comes from adversity. It defines the human experience. It is important to see that life can be reduced to one simple aspect: free choice. The difference between the poor and the rich is simply choice. If you understand that your life path just boils down to your choosing financial freedom or not, then my work is done. You have no need to read any further, as my intent is not to just write a "how to book" but rather to ignite within your spirit a spark to strive for financial freedom. You must choose to be rich every day. You can come up with reasons or excuses for why you can't or don't achieve your goals, but the road to financial freedom is there if you choose it. You don't need this book or any other to teach you how to be wealthy. Believe it or not, you already are. There is no secret to being rich. Your real Rich Dad has already planted that seed within you. You must simply discover it, nurture it, and, most importantly, respect it.

Kiyosaki's book helped me shine light on my seed: to share my passion for rising above adversity and succeeding. You will find your own seed and unlock its potential to create unlimited wealth in your life. Unlike the authors of other real-estate investment books I have read, I feel as though it is important to share this part of myself with you. People are all multifaceted, and no one exists or functions in isolation. To achieve financial growth, it is also necessary to achieve social and spiritual growth. These and many more facets combine to form individuals' personalities. I hope this illustration of my driven spirit is an inspiration to yours.

Wouldn't it be a shame to just let all of that inspiration go to waste? Oh, believe me, it's quite easy to fall into that trap. After all, it has taken me years to write this book. But listen very carefully, be careful about who you listen to. This not only applies to people whose advice you request but also to those who freely volunteer it. At times those who freely volunteer it end up being negative people that hinder us on our path to success.

The techniques I share in this book are not just textbook techniques but methods I have learned from reading books, attending seminars, completing home-study courses, and pursuing a variety of my very own life experiences. These techniques are the same techniques that I have used in purchasing numerous real-estate properties. I currently have a one-hundred-unit apartment complex, a U.S. post office, and several one- and two-unit homes and condos in my portfolio. I also own a grocery store and a restaurant-franchise location of a new health food chain in Manhattan, and I'm also a partner in a music company. With the launch of this book, I will be the proud owner of a new book publisher. So again I caution you, be careful whom you listen to and evaluate what qualifies that person to give you "expert" advice.

Chapter 6

Crabs in a Pot

Have you heard of the "crabs in a pot" theory? Picture a huge pot of boiling water on a stove. The chef has a crate of live fresh crabs that must be boiled to perfection for avid seafood lovers. As the chef places the crabs in the pot, he makes a rather chilling observation. As one crab tries to escape the pot, a crab below it will reach up with its sharp claws to pull the first crab down, thinking that pulling the escaping crab will enable its unfortunate self to take its place on the route to freedom. This vicious cycle continues with each escaping crab, so not one crab escapes. They all remain in the pot, boiling their way to the dinner plate. They fight until the end, never realizing that they share the same fate and that the "every crab for itself" mentality is what guarantees their demise. They never work together as a team to come up with a way to climb out of the pot to safety.

Now picture an active ant hill. These small creatures engineer amazing, complex systems to move objects ten times their own weight. They create assembly lines that are efficient in time saved and in work completed. These ants use the assemblies to build their hills and to provide food for the colony. In the presence of danger, their natural reactions in the fight or flight syndrome still work systematically—they stick together and fight together.

Humans can learn a lot from the crabs' mistakes and the ants' successes. Unfortunately, most people walk around with a crab's mentality. Therefore, I caution you, be careful of whom you listen to. You may become excited as you read this book, and the moment that the spark of inspiration is ignited in your heart, one of the first things you'll do is tell someone about the investment you're planning to make. I guarantee you that more than half the people you tell will voice some unsolicited negative opinion about your capabilities or your venture.

Don't listen to these people—they're the crabs in the bottom of the pot. So your first Life Assignment is to develop your "Crab List." Think about all the people in your circle of influence with whom you speak on a regular basis, such as your family, friends, and co-workers. When you think about each person individually, consider that person's "crab potential." On a scale of 1 to 5, rate each person as to how likely he or she is to pull you down in the pot (1) or to help you try to escape (5). Anyone who gets rated 1, 2, or 3 should be listed in the "Bad Crab" column of your list. Place people rated 4 and 5 in the "Good Crab" column. You don't have to worry about the Good Crabs, as these are the people who are supportive of you, even if they have no clue what you are doing or are about to attempt. They offer you encouragement when you need it at the most crucial crossroads in your investing, they provide you with nonjudgmental listening ears when you need them, and sometimes they even volunteer themselves as resources to help you accomplish whatever is necessary to achieve your goals. They are not selfish, envious, or jealous that you're a crab trying to escape the pot and instead want to do everything in their power to help you make that great escape.

The Bad Crabs are those people who "decrease" you and your goals. Most of these crabs don't act maliciously but rather are sad and miserable people who can never imagine your being successful because they can't imagine *themselves* being successful. Misery loves company, and you've been in the presence of their company for far too long for you to think you can just leave them to wallow in their pity party. They are negative in their day-to-day thought processes, sit around waiting for opportunities to happen rather than creating them, and have no problem blaming everyone else and everything around them for their current sad states of being instead of realizing that they are their own biggest obstacles.

Life Assignment 1: Crab List

Vision: Complete the list below of people you talk to on a regular basis. On the "Good Crab" column list those people who "increase" your life and on the "Bad Crab" column list those people who "decrease" your life. Being able to identify the personality traits of the people around you will help you control the impact of their comments.

Bad Crab	Good Crab
1.	1.
2.	2.
3.	3.
4.	4.
5.	5.
6.	6.
7.	7.

In getting your house in order, you have to start with the emotional clutter. Look at the crabs on your list and evaluate whether you should continue your current relationships with these people, remove them completely from your life, or filter the information you tell them—not for their sakes, but for yours. Those crabs whom you know deep down are Bad Crabs with malicious intent must be cut off. Your current relationship with them is detrimental to your financial freedom. If you take this step, you will hate me now but love me later. You don't need those negative comments and vibrations in your life. Do some housekeeping and get rid of them. Some people will be easier than others to minimize your interactions with. For those crabs that are closer to you like a relative you may have to let what they say go in one ear and out the other. You may not be able to choose your family but you can certainly mentally filter what they say and how it affects you. Remember, if a person is not increasing you, he or she is decreasing you. Surround yourself with positive, likeminded people as you pursue your goals.

This decision is actually what inspired me to form my own cash-flow club. Once I got inspired to do something different with my life, I bought the *Rich Dad* book for six of my closest friends. I was amazed that when it came to making plans regarding what club we were going to party at on Friday night, everyone was down for it. But when it came to my talking about buying an investment property or starting a business, the level of enthusiasm was not the same. I realized that I had a certain group of people who were only good for hanging out; another group of people with whom I could have intellectually stimulating conversations about the stock market, real estate, and so forth; and a third group of people who played hard but also worked hard when the time was right.

So I purchased the book for six of my friends, because I didn't want them to sit around and become jealous of my success. I wanted them to be afforded the same opportunities I had by reading the book, thus creating the chance for us to grow together as we started our quests for financial freedom. Needless to say, some of my friends were inspired and worked to move themselves closer to financial freedom, but most didn't (and I no longer hang out with those who didn't). I didn't let my friends' reactions stop me from pursuing my dream. I needed to surround myself with like-minded people, so I started the Rich Dad cash-flow club for purely selfish reasons: to serve as a sounding board for my ideas. The only requirements to be a member of the club are that you have to have read Rich Dad, Poor Dad and that you share with someone else whatever you learn in the group. I require prospective members to have read Kiyosaki's book because then I know they have opened themselves up to a new way of thinking about financial freedom. The club has been a great source of Good Crabs in my life.

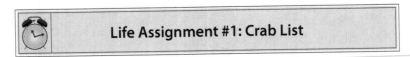

Life Assignment #1: Crab List

Whenever you see a clock in this book, it means you should stop reading exactly where you are and go complete a Life Assignment. Once you have completed it, you can pick right back up where you left off. Now go . . . run off and complete your first assignment. I'll be right here waiting for you when you return . . . .

If you've completed your Crab List and have hardly anyone listed in the "Bad Crab" column, you're just too nice and not really thinking objectively about the negative effect some of the people in your circle of influence have on you. The fact that you are reading this book indicates you have an entrepreneurial spirit. However, the need to whet your appetite for success didn't just happen overnight. It has always been inside you, and you've likely had ideas time and again about businesses you wanted to start that never came to fruition. So if you don't have at least three people listed in your "Bad Crab" column, you need to immediately complete the next Life Assignment, "Discovering the Real You." And if you have three or more people listed in your "Bad Crab" column, that's great, but you still need to complete the next Life Assignment, because it will yield valuable information to help you later.

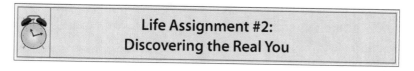

Life Assignment #2:
Discovering the Real You

I'm ashamed of you. I can't believe that I asked you to just take a few minutes and complete a life assignment and you decided not to be authentic and not play full out. It's called a life assignment for a reason. The objective is to change your life. You've been doing the same thing over and over again with no results coming out of it. Don't you think it's about time for a change? I know you must be exhausted. You're stuck in the rat race and these assignments will help you get out. I want you to understand that this book isn't just a concept book or a "how-to" book but a "lets get it done" book and I'm here to do it with you.

So if you decided to be dishonest with yourself and not do the life assignment as I asked you to do then please go back and complete it. I'll be right here waiting for you . . . really . . . I will. If you did do it when you were asked to, I thank you for being authentic and deciding to play full out. You are truly committed and determined to be successful and have gotten off of the sidelines and into the game. It's for you . . . not for me and I'm glad you realized the value of this information. You've paid pennies for this book in comparison to the priceless information that took years for me to learn that I will now share with you.

It is time to go over your completed Life Assignment, "Discovering the Real You." The goal is to evaluate your appetite for risk. Who were you? Who are you now? Are you still living in the same place? If you were renting ten years ago during one of the best housing markets that ever existed and are still renting today, you didn't take advantage of the situation as you could have. Why not? Think about all the money you've thrown away on rent since then. I'm a landlord, so personally I love folks like you for making me richer, but as an educator, I want you to own your own home. For argument's sake, say your rent is $850 per month. Over the past ten years, you have thrown away over $102,000. You likely don't even take a home-office deduction on your taxes or employ other little neat accounting tricks to save some cash, so you've just thrown that money out the window. If you purchased a home ten years ago and are still living in it, why aren't you dreaming a bigger dream? You need to dream big, as your dreams will build your reality. Without dreams, your little choo-choo train of ideas will run out of steam and eventually stall when you hit bumps in the road to financial freedom. This book discusses how to develop these dreams later, but for now, this assignment's purpose is to help you identify areas for improvement.

Consider your employment situation. If you're still working in the same position that you were ten years ago, by the time you finish this book, you'll be on your way to a new, exciting, ever-changing, challenging career that brings you so much joy, you'll hardly be able to stand it. But when I give this assignment in my seminars, I find that because of the global recession, a lot of people say that they were working in fast-paced careers but now find themselves unemployed, living off their savings (if they had any) and praying Congress extends their unemployment benefits. Aren't you tired of having someone else control your destiny? You bought into the dream that you would be loyal and dedicated to your company, and it would be loyal and dedicated to you in return, allowing you to retire after forty years or so of employment—and then the dream dissolved before your eyes. Heck, some folks have seen their entire pension plans disintegrate with no punishments for their employers. Is this your situation?

Look at your income. You're making more money now then you were ten years ago, right? Of course you are! Your company has been nice enough to give you pay raises just sufficient to keep you happy and gainfully employed for it. But if you look at the rate of inflation compared to your salary increases over the past ten years, you'll figure out that you're barely surviving and most likely really living off credit. I want this situation to change for you so your income outpaces—no, *outraces*—inflation and other economic factors. This change can only happen if you're in business for yourself.

Finally, compare who you are now versus who you will be in the future. If you think you will be working in a higher position at your current firm or at your dream company, you chose the *wrong* answer. You need to dream *bigger*. Decide that in the future, you'll be the owner of a company. If you currently own a company, say that you'll be the owner of a new company or will run the parent company of several subsidiaries. Perhaps you'll grow your current $1-billon company into a $5-billion company. Play a bigger game by dreaming a bigger dream.

Chapter 7

Your Mind Is Playing Tricks on You

Leading my cash-flow group discussion is an amazingly insightful experience for me. I get to see members' reactions and hear their voices as they discover their superhuman powers. The group has more than six hundred registered members from around the country, and usually thirty to forty people attend the monthly meeting. It is astounding that so few people attend in comparison to the number of registered local members. I used to think it was a direct reflection on my leadership: why couldn't I keep these people motivated on their path to get out of the rat race? Then I remembered something my stepmother told me when comparing the personal growth of her own children: "everyone grows at their own pace." Some flowers blossom sooner than others. The great thing is that although they may not grow as fast as desired, at least they are growing, and that's positive. In leading my group, I've also noticed that when something is *free*, people don't have a way to place a value on it. The group gives away priceless knowledge, but because members don't pay to be in the group, most can't realize and appreciate the group's true value and only attend meetings occasionally. But that's okay—if the group can just change one's person's life by helping him or her achieve financial freedom, all the time and energy invested will have been worthwhile.

Unlike the face-to-face human interaction I get from leading my group, sitting here writing this book is a new experience for me. I do not know whether you, the reader, are younger or older, male or female, highly educated, rich or poor, just starting out as an entrepreneur or already in business, and so forth. This situation presents a challenge for me, because when I give my talks, I usually start off the session by going around the audience and randomly asking an attendee's first name, how he or she heard about the seminar, the attendee's current profession, and what the person expects to get out of the seminar. This helps me get to know my audience and the direction the seminar should go in. But by working with you through this book, I don't have that luxury—and it's great.

It's sort of like playing Kiyosaki's Cashflow 101 game in life. In the beginning, you randomly choose an occupation—administrative assistant, lawyer, doctor, engineer, teacher, and so forth. The great thing about the game is that it doesn't matter who you currently are: everyone has the same unlocked potential to be winners. In this book, I give you keys to help you turn that lock. Thus, I am writing this book from the framework that because I don't know where you personally are in your investing career, I must provide useful information that will be relevant to novice as well as to expert investors.

This book is an account of my "how to." After reading *Rich Dad, Poor Dad,* I asked myself, "What's next?" What should be my first step, and the next step, and the step after that to achieve personal financial freedom? Maybe this reaction was just my own, or perhaps it was Kiyosaki's intent for his readers. If the latter is true, that was a stroke of genius, because it would prompt readers to investigate an array of additional offerings from his company to further their financial educations (at a price, of course).

Because I'm not privy to any character information about you, I've got to start off by assuming that your mind is open to endless possibilities. The process starts with some heavy-lifting mind-training exercises. You've already completed the first one by creating your Crab List and deciding how to get rid of those Bad Crabs in your life.

Now I need to know your view on money. What is the difference between "poor" people and "rich" people? What is the difference between "rich" people and "wealthy" people? Take a few minutes to really think about how you perceive and define these groups of people.

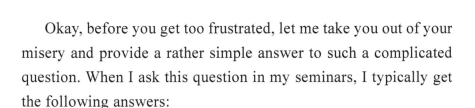

Okay, before you get too frustrated, let me take you out of your misery and provide a rather simple answer to such a complicated question. When I ask this question in my seminars, I typically get the following answers:

- Rich people are just lucky.
- Poor people didn't go to school.
- Wealthy people have more money than rich people.
- Poor people have to work too hard.
- Rich people are on the inside of the deal.
- Wealthy people are like Oprah.

The real difference between rich people and poor people is fear. Rich people are not afraid to take risks. Look at Donald Trump: he has been bankrupt more than once, but he's still investing and moving forward. Why did it take me two years after reading *Rich Dad, Poor Dad* to act upon what the book inspired me to do? As an engineer, I was too smart for my own good. In analyzing potential investments, I wanted to know every variable and calculate every risk. What if this happens? What if that happens? What if the tenant doesn't pay his or her rent? What if the toilet breaks? What if I get sued? What if the place catches fire? What if my credit is bad and I can't qualify for the mortgage to buy the property? My list of excuses went on and on. Did you catch the key word here? *Variable*. Every question I had involved at least one variable, far too many for me to account for in any equation when evaluating the investment risk. The great thing this book teaches is that although you may try your best, you can't control these variables. But if you follow the book's basic principles, you will have mechanisms in place to help you deal with them.

I'll never forget what my father told me during one of my agonizing calls to him as I picked his brain about my list of "what if's." He said I had to be like the Nike commercial and "Just Do It." So I did. I finally stopped making up horror stories in my mind that were bound to happen once I purchased my first real-estate investment property. All those nightmares resulted from my fear.

Periodically in this book, I'll give you a key, the key to help you unlock the success that's buried deep inside. So when you see a "key," that means the information is something very important that I want you to know backward and forward. I'll say it again: *I want you to know it.* I've found that when I really want to know something, I need to write it down a couple of times. You know how the teacher would give you detention if you got in trouble and you would have to write one hundred times on the board, "I will not talk in class" (or whatever your offense was)? This repetition is the same principle. For me, repeatedly writing something down on paper engraves it into my subconscious mind until I'm ready to recall the information when I need it. In essence, that's what the pill did in the movie *Limitless*, as it allowed the main character to recall information buried deep in his brain. You don't have to write this book's "keys" down one hundred times, but do something concrete that will help you remember them and engrave them into your subconscious mind.

> *All you need to* **know** *... is that you will never* **know** *... everything there is to* **know** *... and once you* **know** *that ... you can move on!*

Did you notice how many times the word "know" appears in the key? The word is in bold text so it is superobvious. The word "know" relates to "knowledge," which means education, and even with all the education in the world, you couldn't control all the variables that would keep you from failing in your investments. So the only knowledge you need to have is the means to take action. With that said, go back and read the key a couple of times.

No, I did not have ten shots of tequila when writing that key. It sounds convoluted, yet at the same time it is a strangely profound idea. Let me simplify it for you. Fear stems from not knowing the unknown. Because "the unknown" is also the definition of a variable, why are you racking your brain so much trying to figure everything out? Just let it go. I'll give you tools to help you take not just any risk but a calculated risk. Because you know very little about and have less control over your personal variables, don't let them be the source of fear that keeps you from taking your first step toward success. Once you realize that you can't control the variables, they can no longer control you. Take them out of your thought process and overcome your fear.

Now that this important key has been written in your subconscious, it is time to continue with the mind-training exercises. I've come to the realization that my personal fear was not the fear of failure but the fear of success. I was more into "keeping up with the Joneses" while growing up, and I certainly wanted to look good. So if I thought I might be one of those crabs that could escape the pot, what would my friends say and think about me? "He thinks he's better than everyone else." Stewing over these worries was rather dumb, but I was young and have since grown wiser. But this mental state of being is the inspiration for the next key:

Live in the world of abundance and not scarcity!

Poor people work so hard to get what they have that they worry that no more is available or, if they lose it, regaining what they have lost will be too hard. Often they don't want to let other people know what they have, as they're afraid it might get taken away or that those people will go and get what they already have. Grasping on to things for dear life is actually the death of their entrepreneurial spirit. Rich people live in a world that includes plenty to go around, and if they lose anything, it's easily obtained again. Why? Because they already know how to get it. Statistically, most entrepreneurs fail repeatedly before they find their niches at businesses they're really good at. It's not that hundredth but rather that hundredth-and-first try in which it all just kicks in gear, and the entrepreneur becomes successful. But if this person had given up after ninety-nine attempts, he or she would never have experienced success. So as a poor person, I wasn't afraid of being a failure but of being successful, how it would look on me, and how I would handle it with my friends. I'm so glad that I now wear success well.

I've also come to the realization that the only true failure lies in not trying. The mere fact that you've tried a venture makes you successful, because the knowledge you gained from that experience was priceless. You couldn't pay enough money in any higher-learning institution to gain the information that you personally experience while going through a foreclosure, bankruptcy, lawsuit, and so forth. You learn and grow from these experiences and bring their knowledge with you to your next ventures, so embrace them. Take even a negative experience and turn it positive. The experience is priceless.

But back to my original question (which I haven't forgotten): the difference between rich people and wealthy people is that wealthy people give back unconditionally. I'll say it again: give and it shall be given up on to you. In fact, this idea is the inspiration for a key:

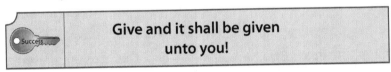

Give and it shall be given unto you!

I'm not saying that rich people are not giving people, as they generally are. But wealthy people make donations on a much grander scale. They are philanthropists. They've realized a higher calling to purpose in their lives and work daily to help improve the world. I say if you want to be wealthy, start while you're poor. Work "giving" into the equation, whether by tithing, volunteering, and so forth, but do something that allows you to give back.

The final reconditioning exercise involves how you view your resources. Take a minute to think about them. Which are your two most precious resources?

Have you heard of the acronyms "OPM" and "OPT"? They represent "Other People's Money" and "Other People's Time," respectively. Time and money are your most valuable resources. However, I say only one resource is truly precious, and that's time. You can't create or control time, so you must use it wisely. The tools and techniques I give you in this book are designed to help you work smarter, not harder, so you can make the best use of your time. Condition your mind to think in measurements of time, not money.

Occasionally, read this mind-reconditioning section to retrain your mind regarding how you view yourself and your money. Being in the right state of mind is the first step you need to take before starting your investment. Without a strong mind, overcoming the challenges that will arise will be very difficult.

Chapter 8

Getting Your House in Order

Before you begin your financial heavy lifting, you really need to know where you are. Without knowing where you are and where you want to go, you cannot map out a route to financial freedom. This quest requires taking a quantitative approach—emotion has no place in investing.

Getting your house in order means getting prepared for success. As part of the process of cleaning up the clutter in your life, you need to examine your credit and your financial statements.

Reviewing your credit is the most painful part of this entire process. Most people would rather get root canals than look at their credit reports. I assume that you are currently credit challenged, as are most people who attend my seminars. As I write this book, the United States (and many other countries) is going through economic turmoil following the recession with many people losing their jobs and homes.

Let's start with the credit basics. When you are applying for financing, lenders typically consider three factors: (1) your willingness to repay the debt (credit), (2) your ability to repay the debt (income), and (3) how much you have at stake in the deal (pledged assets). In the mortgage industry, exotic products were created that totally ignored the income and assets portion of the lending criteria, so financing approval was solely based on applicants' credit scores. That insanity greatly contributed to the global recession. Consequently, the people responsible have made it even more difficult for future business owners like you and me to get access to capital, but that's why you're reading this book and getting prepared. Credit standards have gotten stricter; whereas you used to only need a 680 credit score to obtain business lending, in today's climate you need a 740. Wait . . . 680 . . . 740 . . . what the heck do these numbers mean?

Credit scores range from 300 to 900. Three credit agencies— Experian, TransUnion, and Equifax—use mathematical models to generate these scores. Each has its own proprietary model to generate your score based on credit-history information collected on you. Because the scoring model is different for each agency, the lender chooses which score to use. Some lenders will take the middle score as your credit score for lending. For example, if your three scores are 720 (Experian), 740 (TransUnion), and 800 (Equifax), the lender will use 740 as your score. Some lenders only pull credit reports from one agency. Many business-lending institutions tend to use Experian as their agency of choice. Some lenders will use an average of the three, so in this example, your score would be 753 for lending purposes. Regardless of the method used, in today's market, it's safe to say that you'll need at least a score of 740 to employ the techniques I describe in this book to build your business.

What if you don't know your credit score? You should always

look at your credit report twice a year to make sure it is free of errors that could negatively impact your score. The Fair Credit Reporting Act (FCRA) allows you to obtain one free credit report every twelve months. Visit http://www.AnnualCreditReport.com to get your free report, although you'll have to pay a fee to get your score. If your score is not at least 740, your options are to hire a company or to attempt do-it-yourself credit repair or to bring another partner with good credit into the deal to apply for financing for you.

The concept of using OPM often means seeking a bank loan, but without meeting the minimum credit score, financing is difficult. Your score could mean automatic denial or approval but with high interest rates for the capital. However, with the investing techniques I describe, interest rates are not a factor in determining whether or not you should proceed with an investment. Everyone can obtain financing somehow—the question is how much will it cost you to do so? The higher the credit score, the cheaper the money. But don't let bad credit stop you from pursuing a deal.

Bad credit is often an indicator of money mismanagement. If this describes your situation, start repairing your credit now and learn from your mistakes. Life is much more enjoyable when you don't have the dark cloud of bad credit hanging over your head. Use what you have learned from your past credit mistakes to help you run your future business successfully.

If your middle credit score is below 720, get a copy of my e-book *Let's Build: Excellent Credit* from http://www.CEOeBooks.com to help you repair your credit problems and to improve your score. It is too much information to include in this book. For now, just check your credit report and score to ensure that no errors exist and to know where you stand.

Now it is time to talk about your money. This Life Assignment, "Financial Statements," will help you learn about your money as you complete the following worksheets: (1) Income Statement, (2) Balance Sheet, (3) Cost of Capital, and (4) Working Money. These worksheets will play a crucial role in mapping your road to financial freedom.

Life Assignment #3: Financial Statements
Download at http://www.CEOeBooks.com

The Income Statement provides a snapshot of your monthly income and your monthly expenses. You will probably experience a rude awakening when you fill it out, because when most of my seminar attendees complete this worksheet, they instantly realize they have negative monthly cash flows. How is this possible? You are most likely supplementing your monthly income with credit, savings, or a combination of both. If this describes you, you're living way above your means. Carefully review Section D to determine which living expenses you can cut back on or eliminate to bring your expenses in line with your income. Also determine how much you have in liquid reserves, or how much you have saved in cold cash to pay your monthly living expenses. Ideally, you should have a reserve of at least six months of living expenses in cash or liquid investments on hand in case your income were to stop (for example, if you were laid off or had a temporary medical problem).

The Balance Sheet shows your current net worth and leveraging power of your assets to purchase more assets. You probably have a negative net worth, perhaps because an asset whose purchase you financed has decreased in current market value so much that you owe more for the asset than its worth. Many people have experienced price drops in their home values, so now they owe more for their houses than what they are worth. And, of course, a car starts to depreciate in value the moment you drive it off the lot, so you may owe more on your car loan today than the vehicle's Kelley Blue Book value.

The Cost of Capital sheet is very important and is often overlooked by financial planners when taking your financial snapshot. It shows how much you are being charged for your current debt. And in fact, as you realized after filling out the Balance Sheet, most of the assets you have purchased are not really assets but liabilities. An "asset" is something that puts money into your pocket, and a "liability" is something that takes money out of your pocket. So I have news for you: that flatscreen TV that you purchased using a store card last Christmas was a big whopping liability and not the asset you convinced yourself it was. And that introductory period of six months with 0 percent interest has ended and kicked the interest rate up to 22 percent. That's why this spreadsheet is a great starting point when reorganizing your debt to help increase your monthly cash flow. Call your creditors to ask if they are offering any balance-transfer specials. If you qualify, transferring a balance from a higher-interest-rate credit card to one with the special rate being offered will save you money. You should know some credit-score-maintenance techniques before making the transfer, so refer to *Let's Build: Excellent Credit* for more information before moving your debt around. You also should call up each creditor and ask to have your interest rate reduced. If the representative advises that this can't be done, ask to speak with a supervisor. Repeat the request to have your interest rate reduced, saying that another lender is offering a lower rate, and you're sure that your current creditor wouldn't appreciate losing you as a customer. If you have extra room in your new budget to pay more than the minimum on any account, choose the account that has the highest interest rate to work on paying off first. The goal is to get to $0 of bad debt.

The Working Money sheet spotlights your current rate of return on your liquid assets. Look at the interest rate you're getting on each account, and think about how you can move the money around. Your money should be working as hard as it can for you, not the other way around. Use such great sites as http://www.Bankrate.com to check for higher-interest-rate checking and savings accounts and CDs in addition to lower-interest-rate credit cards.

A great Web site that I use to keep track of all my assets and liabilities is http://www.Mint.com. It allows me with to see a snapshot of my balance sheet with one log in. It also analyzes my spending patterns and makes suggestions regarding where I can save. You can also set up budgets on the site that help you monitor your spending habits. If your cell-phone bill is outrageous, use http://www.BillShrink.com to look for ways to save on it as well.

Chapter 9

Your Outside World Is a Reflection of Your Inside World

Now that you've worked on cleaning up your mental clutter, it's time to work on your physical clutter. The TV show *Hoarders* illustrates just how much stuff people can accumulate and get accustomed to living with..

A life coach once told me, "Your outside world is a reflection of your inside world." So far, you've worked to declutter your thoughts, people in your circle of influences, and problem areas in your finances. You should feel good about what you've already accomplished, but the tremendous high you feel can come crashing down if you have a chaotic mess in your home.

Clean sweeping is not one of my strong suits, and (as I discuss earlier in this book) you should be careful whom you listen to. Because home-office organization is not my area of expertise, I won't attempt to advise you beyond saying that if your office is a mess, stop reading now to clean it up and get it organized.

Life Assignment #4: Home Office Space

As you sit in your office and work to build your business, a clean, organized environment will help keep your thoughts flowing. If necessary, search online for professional home organizers to come and organize everything for you if you're not capable or willing to do so, but make sure you have a clean and harmonious working space.

EASY STEP

Finding Your "I" in Passion

"If there is no passion in your life, then have you really lived? Find your passion, whatever it may be. Become it, and let it become you and you will find great things happen FOR you, TO you and BECAUSE of you."

—T Alan Armstrong

Chapter 10

Work? What Is Work?

Y ou're off to a great start in getting your finances in order, so now it's time to do a little more soul searching. To really live, you need to know what makes you tick. When you get paid to do what you love, I don't call it work—I call it life.

So how do you find out what makes you tick? It's a simple question, but most people find it very difficult to answer. Earlier I said that time and money are your two most precious resources, but only time is *really* precious. You can't create time, move it forward or backward, or stop it, but you can certainly create and control your own money. So if you had all the time in the world and all the money in the world, what would you be doing right now? You'll determine your answer in Life Assignment #5, "What Makes You Tick?"

 Life Assignment #5: What Makes You Tick?

Did you find it strange how many things in life interest you? To me, these varied interests are not strange at all—in fact, I expect that to be the case. Human beings are gifted with many different talents and are multifaceted individuals. This variety is what keeps life interesting. I often see such answers as "family," "traveling," "helping people," and "real estate" from people who attend my seminars. I'm pretty ecstatic about most answers, except for my pet peeve: real estate. Many people place real estate on their lists because it's a fad that has been promoted as a "get rich quick" scheme on TV. When I ask these people to revisit their lists, I often find that they are not really passionate about real estate but rather just desperate to make money and to get out of the rat race.

This key is hard to swallow, so get ready: whatever you do in life, do it for love and not for money.

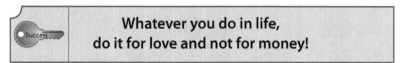

Whatever you do in life, do it for love and not for money!

I know what you're saying to yourself: this is easier said than done when you have money. However, I've learned that when you start to do things in life because you simply love them, the money will come as a byproduct of your passion. I would run my current businesses even if I didn't make one penny from them, just because I love what I do so much. When you do a job only because you're chasing that almighty dollar, the gratification is short lived. True, you may be happy in the interim, but in the long run you won't have the self-gratification to sustain you during those difficult times in the business cycle that will surely come. Wouldn't it be great to do what you love to do and to have people pay you for it? Here's the big revelation of this book: I'm going to take what you would do for free and show you how to make money doing it. No matter what you're passionate about in life, somebody, somewhere—especially in this global market—is just as passionate as you about the same thing and is willing to pay you for your expertise.

A friend told me she had joined a wine club. She pays $30 per month for membership in a group of other wine fanatics. Her membership benefits include having the wine of the month delivered to her doorstep, knowing the best vineyards to visit, participating in local wine tastings, and other perks. She works on Wall Street, and after spending exhaustive hours on the trading desk, she doesn't have the time to do her own research to stay abreast of the best wines in the market (Reminder: Your two most precious resources are time and money). And because she doesn't have the time to put into her passion, she's willing to invest her money with someone who *does* have the time and is just as passionate about wine as she is. As a nondrinker, I would have thought this club was a harebrained idea, because drinking wine is not my passion. But a wine lover in Brooklyn developed the concept and has created an online business that delivers multiple income streams generated from membership subscriptions and advertising, all with low start-up costs.

Has the lightbulb over your head turned on yet? Yes, you, too, can take any idea and turn it into a cash cow for yourself. And yes, it's okay to have more than one passion. You just need to prioritize the things that you're passionate about and start with the one about which you're *most* passionate. The original title of this book was *Finding Your "I" in Passion*, because "passion" is spelled with an "I," and that "I" represents who you are and the business you're trying to build. The way you do this is to create your "I" out of your passions listed in Life Assignment #5.

First, decide what you're most passionate about in life. So go back to your worksheet from Life Assignment #5. Now it is time to fill in the "Happy" column that had been left blank. Review your list and rank each one of your passions, numbering them from "1" (what you're most passionate about) downward. The "Happy" factor means that doing the number-one thing on your list makes you happier than anything else.

Now, convert your passion into a business. In the "Conversion" column on the worksheet, think of the type(s) of business you could develop from your passion. Here's an example:

Life Assignment 5: What makes you tick?

Vision: This exercise will help you to discover what you're truly passionate about in life. Just read and answer the question and write down each activity as it pops in your mind. Don't worry about the happy & conversion column for now you'll fill that in later.

Question: If time and money were not a factor, what would you be doing right now? That means if you had all the time in the world and all the money in the world what are things you'd do that make you happy?

Answers	Happy	Conversion
Traveling	6	Travel Guide
Spending time with Family	5	Recreational Center
Helping People	1	Homeless Shelter
Reading Books	3	Book Club
Baking Cakes	2	Bakery
Playing Video Games	4	Game Rating/Review
_____	__	_____
_____	__	_____
_____	__	_____
_____	__	_____
_____	__	_____
_____	__	_____

In this example, you may wonder how turning "Helping People" into the business of a "Homeless Shelter" will allow someone to make money. Yes, this should be a nonprofit business, but even owners of nonprofits can still make money, so it could still be a viable business choice. Review your list now and brainstorm the types of businesses you could start under the "Conversion" column.

Chapter 11

Be a Good PIG Farmer

L et me show you my "I" and tell you about it before you create
your own.

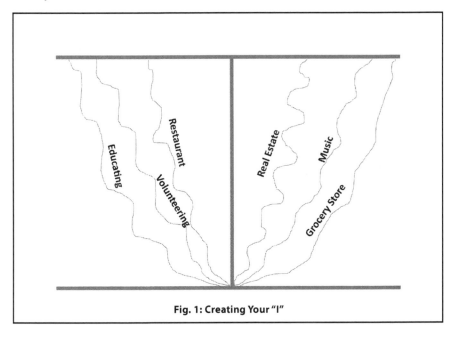

Fig. 1: Creating Your "I"

I have several Passive Income Generators (PIGs) in my "I." If you take care of your PIGs, your PIGs will take care of you. If a farmer wants to be profitable, he or she probably wouldn't be able to do so with just one pig—it would require having several pigs. So model yourself after a good farmer, and nurture your PIGs. This concept will be discussed in more detail later when I talk about how to run several companies at the same time.

Many people who attend my seminar tell me they own a business. I ask them one simple question: *"Can you go to Tahiti for a year and still make money?"* Oftentimes they go quiet, and I know immediately that means the answer is "no." That's because they work and work and work, but instead of working for someone else's company, they slave away for themselves. Just because you're self-employed does not mean you are a true business owner as I define it for the purposes of achieving financial freedom. You're still dedicating the majority of your time to working in your business. If you weren't there, would your business still thrive without you?

It would be humanly impossible for me to dedicate all my time to working in each PIG I own. Until scientists figure out how to clone me, the next best thing is for me to have management teams in place to do my job. I function as the CEO of all my companies and spend my day reviewing information and providing feedback for each as problems arise, but I can do that from my laptop in Tahiti, and it usually only takes about an hour out of my day. Work . . . what work? I call it retirement, and that's how I know I am financially free. Isn't life wonderful?

What I want you to do now is to complete Life Assignment #6, "Creating Your 'I.'" Do not place any business on the solid line that forms the "I." Instead, place one business on each squiggly line. You may have listed several businesses when you completed Life Assignment #5, but that's why I had you go back and assign a "Happy" factor to each one to help you prioritize them. With that said, do not list more than six businesses on your "I."

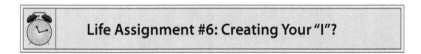

Life Assignment #6: Creating Your "I"?

Financial freedom must be defined quantitatively, and to do that you'll use the financial statements you completed earlier when you were cleaning up your clutter. Your passive income is money that works for you as opposed to your working for it. You may be earning interest on your checking account, money-market account, or CDs, but this income is not generated from business activities. Thus, you're probably starting out with $0 as your passive income from businesses—and that's great. I love people who are starting with nothing, because their minds are open to endless possibilities and are not jaded from their past experiences. In this example, as a CEO-to-be, you are just starting out, so place $0 at the bottom line of the "I." Suppose you have a total of $5,000 of monthly living expenses as calculated on your Income Statement. Place $5,000 on the top line of the "I." Now you know the starting point and the defining point for you to achieve financial freedom.

The road to financial freedom oftentimes isn't an easy one, but it is quite fun. Look at the figure for my "I." Notice that I did not place a business on the straight line that connects the top and bottom lines. That's because in my experience, I have not found building a company to be easy or an overnight success. It takes

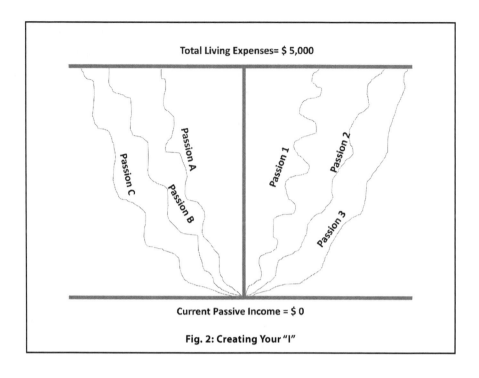

Total Living Expenses= $ 5,000

Current Passive Income = $ 0

Fig. 2: Creating Your "I"

some heavy lifting and time, but the process is enjoyable along the ride to the top. I placed each of my businesses on squiggly lines, because the road to freedom is a winding road that is ever turning, and each turn represents a roadblock that must be overcome to continue on the path to success. That's why one of the most important keys in this book states that whatever you do must be done for love and not money. If you do not love what you do, when these roadblocks come—and trust me, they will—you'll easily give up on your goals. If you are pursuing your true love, your passion, you will find a way under, over, around, or through those roadblocks so you can continue on your path to success. I guarantee you the roadblocks will come. Some will be small potholes in the road, and some will be enormous concrete barricades. Embrace these roadblocks when you encounter them, as they will make you stronger. What you learn from them will be priceless and can never be taught in any classroom or in any book.

Take one last look at my "I." Notice that the squiggly lines never go in the reverse direction. I may veer to the left or veer to the right to get around the roadblocks when I hit them, but I never reverse my path toward my financial-freedom goal. The drive and determination needed for you to bulldoze your way through any obstacle is rooted in your passion. If people hit their first roadblocks and give up, unfortunately their "I" diagrams look a little something like this:

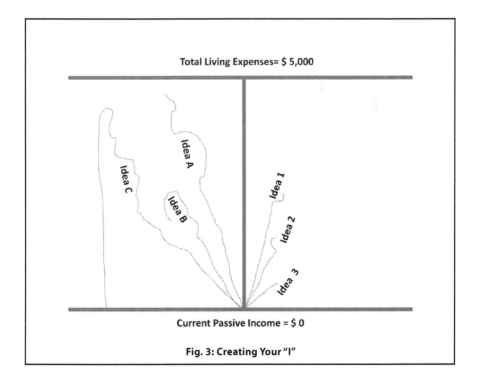

Fig. 3: Creating Your "I"

I've changed the labels from "Passion" to "Idea," as that's all that these business starts were—real passions cannot be stopped and are themselves unstoppable. However, pay close attention to each "Idea." Notice that in this example, the person reached different levels with each idea attempted. In "Idea 1," the entrepreneur's business was moving along successfully but hit a small roadblock; the CEO figured out a solution but then quickly gave up, probably due to emotional stress. When attempting "Idea 2," the CEO was a little more dedicated and overcame a slightly larger roadblock than what he or she faced in "Idea 1," but, as usual, the person gave up. On the person's third attempt to be successful, he was just so emotionally drained from Ideas 1 and 2 that Bad Crabs who were really good at giving unsolicited negative feedback were allowed to infiltrate...and the entrepreneur simply gave up. Again. After some time passed, the would-be business owner was busy working as a dreadful, miserable, unfulfilled employee at someone else's company. (I'm laying it on thick with the adjectives because this level of discontent gets people motivated to get back out there and try to go it alone again.) The entrepreneur decided to give financial freedom another shot. This time, with "Idea A," notice that he got pretty close to achieving financial freedom but gave up as he approached the finish line. Often, you'll find that after hearing "no" ninety-nine times, the hundredth time that you ask finally receives a "yes" response. The lesson here is to not give up. It takes ninety-nine "no's" to get that one "yes," but that one "yes" is all you need. In "Idea B," the entrepreneur had a rather small setback and then gave up. In "Idea C," he got pretty far, but a major setback caused him to simply give up. This poor entrepreneur doesn't need ideas—he needs passions.

Go back to your own "I." Enter your current monthly passive income from your business activities at the bottom, and at the top of your "I" enter your total current monthly living expenses as calculated on your Income Statement. You have now fully defined your "I" and the roads to get you to the finish line. Your "I" shows you the number and types of games you'll be playing, but the great thing about these games is that the grand prize is financial freedom.

Your road to success won't be easy, so I need to give you more tools to help you overcome your roadblocks. Success does not come without commitment. Earlier, you completed your Crab List, placing those individuals who are negative influences in your life in the "Bad Crab" column. I have news for you: oftentimes you are your own worst enemy and the biggest Bad Crab of them all. You create the most powerful negative thoughts, and although you've done some mind-reconditioning exercises earlier in the book (which I encourage you to revisit), you need some daily reminders to help you stay positive and focused.

Chapter 12

Cheat Sheet for Your New Game

You've created some fun new games that you'll be playing full out on your "I" path to financial freedom. Each business on your "I" is a game, and although it usually is not nice to cheat, in this game of life, cheaters do win. You can cheat, because you invented the game and you're making up the rules as you play it. So don't be afraid to attack these games of life head on, as there's no way you can lose, especially with the cheat sheets you're about to create.

I am a firm believer in the power of positive affirmations. I believe that you can speak things into existence. If you say you are successful, you will be successful. If you speak failure into your life, you will be a failure. Reciting positive affirmations moves the positive thoughts from your conscious into your subconscious so, unbeknownst to you, you are continuously working on your goal. The same principle applies to writing something down to remember it. For example, when you have an idea, it's just a loose concept floating around in the universe. The moment you write it down, you pull it from the abstract into the concrete and implant it in your subconscious. With that said, I would like for you to write the following statement in Life Assignment #7, "Creed":

> *I am choosing to have financial freedom in my life. I am committing to having my money work for me rather than working for it myself. I will be dedicated to my passion and to having my passion become the vehicle by which the income generated by my passion exceeds my expenses.*
>
> *I take this oath understanding that it's more than a commitment to my team members; more importantly, it's a commitment to myself. I make this declaration of financial success in my life and will honor my word.*

If you wish, you can paraphrase this creed with your own words that reflect your dream of financial freedom and your commitment to achieving it in your life.

 Life Assignment #7: Creed

Now that you've completed your creed, post it somewhere to serve as a daily reminder to your subconscious. Perhaps taping it to the mirror in your bedroom or bathroom so you see it every morning will work for you, or you could attach it to the back of the front door of your home so you absorb the reminder each day before you go to work.

The second tool that will serve as your daily passion reminder is Life Assignment #8, "Vision Board." Review your worksheet from

Life Assignment #5, "What Makes You Tick?" Look on the Internet or in magazines or books for images that represent your passions. Cut them out and place them on your vision board. For example, say you chose "Traveling" as a passion. Cut out and display picture of exotic places you would like to visit. After you have completed your vision board, display it prominently as a constant reminder of the rewards of financial freedom. Completing this will take some time, so I don't suggest that you stop reading here and immediately complete your board, but don't forget to do this assignment soon. It is deeply important and powerful, and it works.

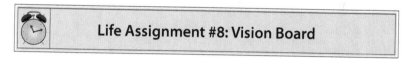

Life Assignment #8: Vision Board

Finally, the last creative power-of-suggestion tool is Life Assignment #9, "Resignation Letter." If you are currently working for someone else, in the words of David Allan Coe performed by Dolly Parton, I want you to tell that person to *"take this job and shove it"*—but not just yet, because first you have to reach the top of your "I" so you can afford to live. Your next assignment is to simply write a resignation letter to your current employer dated sometime in the future. It sounds crazy, but have you heard Jim Carrey's story? Back in 1987, when he was twenty-five years old, he was a struggling comedian trying to break into show business. One night, he drove his old Toyota to the top of the Hollywood Hills. While sitting there, overlooking Los Angeles and daydreaming about his future, he decided to write himself a check in the amount of $10 million and dated Thanksgiving 1995. In the memo section of the check, he wrote *"for acting services rendered.*" By the time Thanksgiving 1995 rolled around, he had starred in *Ace Ventura: Pet Detective*, *The Mask*, and *Dumb & Dumber*, with worldwide box-office revenues reaching $550 million. His price tag for "services rendered" far exceeded what he wrote on the check, as his market value was then up to $20 million per picture. This example illustrates suggestive powerful thinking at its best. He created a goal for himself and planted it in his subconscious mind by writing it down in the form of a check. He worked daily toward his goal to meet his deadline, but not only did he reach his targeted goal, he far surpassed what he had envisioned on that night in 1987. The technique worked for Jim Carrey, and it will work for you. Just pick a date in the future, write a sincere resignation letter, and sign it.

Life Assignment #9: Resignation Letter

Hide this letter somewhere in your workspace not accessible by your co-workers. Every time someone at your job drives you crazy, pull the resignation letter out and read it to yourself. Every time you feel like you've gotten too complacent at work, pull it out then as well. It will be a great motivator to get you back on track toward pursuing your financial-freedom goal.

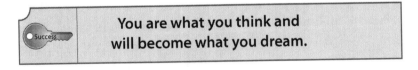

You are what you think and will become what you dream.

Business Basics

---●---

"The greatest barrier to success is the fear of failure."

—Sven Goran Eriksson

Chapter 13

Where Do I Start?

I'm sure at this point you're thinking, "Okay, you've given me all these great tools I'll need for success—but now what?" At least, that's the question I'd be asking the author if I were reading this book.

It's important to start by defining the basics of investing. All the investing you will do should be treated as a business, which is what I'm about to discuss. According to Kiyosaki, that income stream would be a business, real estate, or the market as your PIG. You've identified multiple streams of income, as diagrammed on your "I," and later you will pick one to start with.

For now, I'm going to use the business of real estate to explain basic investing principles. Tangible assets are easier for most people to understand, so I'll use brick-and-mortar structures as examples. Real estate is a broad category that encompasses residential and commercial properties, but my expertise is in HUD foreclosures, so I'll present information from this framework.

Chapter 14

Killing Chicken Little

If you haven't read Kiyosaki's *Rich Dad, Poor Dad,* as I say at the beginning of my book, put this book down and read his work first. Kiyosaki does a fantastic job of explaining how income streams can be generated whether you are an employee, self-employed, a business owner, or an investor. Different tax implications are associated with each, and he beautifully demonstrates why you should choose to be a business owner and investor. These two classifications have the greatest tax benefits and allow you to truly enjoy financial freedom.

The key to financial freedom is having passive-income streams. As I have stated before, instead of your working hard for your money, your money is working hard for you. Financial freedom describes that point at which the income generated from passive streams exceeds your monthly living expenses. This freedom can be achieved through several vehicles, such as dividends from your investment portfolio, independently operating businesses, real-estate investment property, and many more options. I chose real estate as my first stream of passive income. As I write this book (at age thirty-three), I find myself owning more HUD properties than I care to mention. But more importantly, the knowledge I've gained from buying, renovating, and renting these HUD foreclosures has been priceless. I'll mention that I've purchased tax liens, bank foreclosures, and properties on the open market as well, so the concepts in this book can be applied to any type of real-estate investment you're considering.

So how did it all begin? After reading Kiyosaki's book, I did as most of you will probably do after reading this book: I got inspired with confidence, and then I just let all that enthusiasm wither away. I read the book, mentally developed a plan to buy real estate, and then let the fear factor take complete control. As I reflect on that period in my life, I can say that what I really feared most was success. Really, I had nothing to lose and so much to gain. Damn those Bad Crabs!

Kiyosaki warns his readers about the fear of taking risk. This fear engulfed me for nearly two years. Just call me Chicken Little, because I definitely would have said that the sky was falling. Perhaps I was afraid to try my hand at real estate, knowing that it could all go wrong and that I could lose nearly all my hard-earned assets. Perhaps I was scared because I didn't have a mentor to guide me, to hold my hand through the process, to give me much-needed assurance that every calculated step I would take would be the right step. No matter what my reasons were, by themselves, they could never explain why it took me years to act upon the knowledge I accumulated. Today, I welcome risk with open arms. Of course, I still experience fear of the unknown, but the difference is that instead of letting it stop me, this fear propels me full steam ahead to greatness. Now I can identify it, acknowledge its presence, and deal with it accordingly. For example, it took me months to actually sit down and write the first word in this book. However, this time around, my slow start was not because of my fear of success but rather my lack of time. And even now, I'm retraining myself to live a life based on time management, if one can ever really manage time. I think of it as gaining respect for time and treating it as my most precious resource.

This is what I've learned about taking risk: fear is part of the human spirit, part of being human, and part of enjoying the human experience. Living without this emotion is impossible, so realizing that you can coexist with it will make life much easier. You will come to realize that you will never know everything there is to know. Once you accept this limitation, you can move forward in life and take that leap of faith that you have been expending so much exhausting energy to avoid. Sound familiar? As an engineer, I'm trained to calculate. In fact, I am a victim of analysis paralysis. Trying to calculate my risk in an investment and to predict its outcome leads to my overanalyzing that investment. There are too many variables, which is what makes them variables. But if you accept that you can't know everything about an investment, you will reduce that fear to nearly nothing. While I would waste time and energy trying to evaluate a deal from every angle, some other investor would grab it from right under my nose. Of course, you can also learn techniques to help reduce your fear, but they do not completely eliminate that fear of the unknown. So I mandate you right now to just accept it, acknowledge that it exists, and use it to push yourself forward instead of letting it hold you back as it has done in the past.

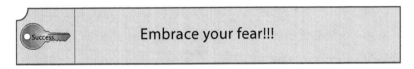

Embrace your fear!!!

The difference between success and failure lies in the way you think. Success results from you affirming that you are successful. People have been programmed to live within the confinements of their own fear. To achieve your boundless potential, you must realize that just by starting out on your venture, you are already successful, and the notion of failure does not exist in your world. The leap of faith you have taken to start the venture gives you priceless knowledge, which in itself is pure success, regardless of whether the outcome of that venture is what you expected.

I consider myself an expert at buying HUD residential-property foreclosures. My proven formula has allowed me to strategically acquire several of these properties. These techniques will also allow you to buy property, regardless of the current state of the real-estate market. Markets will always be in one of three states: (1) up, (2) down, or (3) sideways. The key is identifying which point of the market cycle you're currently in and to invest accordingly. In my world, the market also has a fourth state, which I call the "I don't care" state, because I invest in a way that is profitable regardless of the state of the market. You can find out the step-by-step process in my book *Let's Build: HUD Foreclosure Business* (http://www.CEOeBooks.com).

Chapter 15

Real Estate
Is Our Business

As the cliché goes, the only things that are certain in life are death and taxes. Unless the rules of the world have changed, the only one that's humanly possible to control is taxes. Real estate is definitely one way to control the amount of income tax you pay. More importantly, it's the cornerstone for building wealth in this country and in many others.

Have you ever thought about making the government your business partner? Whether you realize it or not, Uncle Sam already is. As an employee, the government pays itself before you get paid via a nice little concept called "withholding tax." If you haven't paid attention before, take a look at your next pay stub. In many scenarios, the government pays itself 28 percent of your hard-earned money that you worked for every day.

Don't get me wrong—I'm certainly a believer in paying taxes, but not 28 percent. I'm not a fan of the government's "withholding" my wealth. If used properly, taxpayer dollars can be a valuable and essential aspect of the government's operations, but I'll leave the question of proper use of taxes to your imagination. So if you must pay taxes, why not pay as little as possible?

Real-estate investments allow you to legally reduce the amount of income tax you pay. The most popular ways to do this are through phantom depreciation expenses and operating expenses. These investments also allow you to control an appreciating asset while earning income if you performed proper due diligence[1] when purchasing your property. However, the best thing about real estate investing is that, at any point in time, you can sell the property. This available exit strategy provides the biggest relief from that unavoidable and daunting fear factor. Real estate investing does have its risks, but if we are intelligent about our investments, we should be able to reduce these risks to a minimum.

If something sounds too good to be true, then it probably is. You can always come up with "reasons" or "excuses" as to why you aren't successful and why this notion of your being a successful real-estate investor is too far fetched. I've already discussed how to deal with these emotions elsewhere in the book. Embrace your fear.

A later chapter demonstrates some of the tax benefits to owning a business. This information is another tool to add to your arsenal when Bad Crabs try to convince you that you're crazy for wanting to invest in real estate.

Because real-estate investment is such a common business, it works well as the model to build the blueprint in this book, but the concepts I discuss can apply to any business. I want to discuss those concepts now.

---

1 Confirmation of material facts of transaction through reasonable investigation into the physical characteristics, history, tax situation, and any outstanding violations of property.

Chapter 16

The Rule of 3: Asset Litmus Test

R eal-estate investing encompasses several schools of thought. Some people invest for cash flow, to achieve a net loss as it helps to reduce their overall tax burden from other business profits, some invest purely for aesthetic appreciation, and some utilize one of many other strategies. I've studied multiple techniques through books, home-study courses, and seminars. As I did, you must decide which technique is best for you.

I was a victim of information overload after reading *Rich Dad, Poor Dad*. I armed myself with an arsenal of real-estate-investment books. I wanted to know everything there was to know about real estate investing before I invested $1 into a property. However, I studied so much that I found myself in a state of confusion. Should I buy residential or commercial property? Rental property or flips? Open market or foreclosures? The list of unanswered questions went on and on and on.

I finally decided to shut up and get started, plain and simple.

I just had to get in the game and play. I chose to start with rental property. I knew that no matter what type of property I purchased, it would have to pass my litmus test for investing: was it an asset or a liability? I need the property to put money into my pocket every month and not take it out. So many investors who thought they were purchasing an asset found out later that they actually acquired a liability as they didn't do their homework on the deal.

My Rule of 3 requires simply evaluating three financial indicators of a property's cash benefit: (1) positive cash flow, (2) cash-on-cash return on investment (ROI), and (3) appreciation. Not only do I use this rule when evaluating real estate, but I use it for all my investing. These rules will work for any type of business investment you're considering.

Asset Rule #1: Positive Cash Flow

A property's cash flow can exist in one of three states: negative cash flow (–$0), break-even ($0), or positive cash flow (+$0). The cash flow I'm talking about here is really cash flow from operations as defined in the financial world, which is the amount of money left over once the property expenses have been deducted from the rental income. This real, positive cash flow is the amount of your earnings before depreciation,[2] amortization,[3] and noncash charges[4] have been applied. Negative cash flow occurs when you must take money out of your own pocket to help cover the operating expenses on the property. You never want to be in a negative cash-flow position. Remember, generating a revenue stream means making your money work for you instead of your working for your money. It's the money from the positive cash flow you will use for your living

---

2 Reduction in the value of an asset over time.
3 Reduction of the value of an asset by prorating its cost over a period of years.
4 Charge made against earnings that does not involve any cash outlay.

expenses. Break-even occurs when your income just covers your expenses. Your cash flow here is $0, but the potential tax breaks are great benefits, even with break-even properties. However, generating positive cash-flow investments should be your focus.

Here is an example of a cash flow property:

Income

Gross Rental Income	$725
5% Vacancy Reserve	−36
Total Income	$689

Expenses

Mortgage (Principal & Interest)	$540
PMI (Private Mortgage Insurance)	63
Real-Estate Taxes	37
Rental-Dwelling Insurance	20
Management Fee	0
Total Operating Expenses	$660

Cash Flow = Net Rental Income − Total Operating Expenses
= $689 − $660
= $29

Thus, in this example, the monthly positive cash flow is $29. You're investing to make money, not to lose it. This concept is the key to your success. Positive cash flow is the way to reach your goal of being financially free. In *Let's Build: HUD Foreclosure Business* (http://www.CEOeBooks.com), I analyze my HUD foreclosures and provide a spreadsheet to calculate these numbers.

"So, only $29?" you may be saying. You have to be flipping out right now. I know that you can't live off $29 each month, but you know, "Rome wasn't built in a day," and you haven't yet heard about the two other components of the Rule of 3.

Asset Rule #2: Cash-on-Cash ROI

The cash-on-cash ROI is the percentage of income received from the investment divided by the total dollars invested. It's a great tool to use when comparing different investment vehicles or, as I say, "apples to oranges." Suppose you have $1 to invest. Should you invest it in a savings account, a high-yield CD or money-market account, a piece of real estate, a business, stocks, bonds, mutual funds, or futures? The cash-on-cash ROI tells you the percentage of return you'll get for every dollar that you invest across various investment vehicles. For example, suppose you have a 14 percent ROI on a real-estate investment property, a 7 percent return on a particular stock, and a 1.5 percent interest rate on an aggressive savings account. Although each vehicle is completely different, analyzing the ROI levels the playing field to help you choose which investment is right for you. In this example, hands down, the greatest expected return for your investment dollar is real estate.

The way I invest is that I get overexcited, like a little kid opening gifts on Christmas morning. I like to invest with an infinite return on my investment—yes, *infinite*—which means I put no money into the deal but I get money out. How is this possible? It's the concept of OPM at its best. The first method I use to acquire assets is to utilize my unsecured business credit accounts to acquire assets. I'll talk about this later when I discuss leveraging your assets.

If you don't have credit lines to access, use investor loans or other forms of financing for the acquisition costs of your asset.

In real-estate transactions, that's the down payment, closing costs, possible renovation costs, and some small start-up reserves (money set aside for future costs). For example, in the previous example, suppose that you used your unsecured business credit accounts to acquire the asset, and your total monthly payment for the accounts was $10. Here is how your cash flow would now look:

Income

Gross Rental Income	$725
5% Vacancy Reserve	−36
Total Income	$689

Expenses

Mortgage (Principal & Interest)	$540
Acquisition Loan Payment	**10[5]**
PMI (Private Mortgage Insurance)	63
Real Estate Taxes	37
Rental Dwelling Insurance	20
Management Fee	0
Total Operating Expenses	$670

Cash Flow = Net Rental Income − Total Operating Expenses
$$= \$689 - \$670$$
$$= \$19$$

Thus, you've put nothing into this deal ($0), but you're getting $19 per month. You have an infinite ROI. It's like you're not

---

[5] Many people don't consider this cost. Remember that every deal is 100% financed.

showing up to work but still getting paid . . . forever—as long as you control the asset. This beautiful concept is the cornerstone of financial freedom.

Asset Rule #3: Appreciation

The last rule in the litmus test is to evaluate the appreciation potential of your asset. Invest with the hope that sometime in the future, the asset will be worth more than what you paid for it. Above, the returns may appear to be expected appreciation rates, and that may be the case in some instances. But the rates of return used above are really the returns expected on the day you acquire the asset, the return on your initial investment. Because this is speculative regarding the future state of the investment, it should be the last financial indicator considered, even though it is equally important in the overall investment strategy. We will discuss some other examples of this later.

How do you determine the appreciation rate? For real estate, several Internet resources are available to examine historical property prices for cities and neighborhoods. My favorite tool to use is the House Price Index (HPI), published by the Federal Housing Finance Agency (http://www.fhfa.gov). If you're evaluating something on the market, you can likely use tools on your brokerage site for historical evaluations of stocks, bonds, and mutual funds and analyst predictions. For your business, you can also research analyst predictions for the projected growth rate of your industry for the next five years.

Some investors may look at $65 per month as insufficient cash flow. However, it's $65 that you earned without putting in a full day's work at the factory, in the office, or wherever you work. At the same time, your equity in the property should be increasing as you pay your mortgage. It's passive income that puts you further down the road to financial freedom. Your ROI (Return On Investment) in this property should be significantly greater than by letting your money sit in a savings account. You also have the potential to leverage the property by taking the equity out to buy another property or to start a business, not to mention the tax benefits that go with owning this rental property, such as deducting mortgage interest and phantom depreciation.

So dig deep and say goodbye to Chicken Little. Get off the benches and go out on the field to play the game. The game of cash flow is certainly a lot more fun to play when you understand and follow the business basics when acquiring your assets. Use the Rule of 3 to start down the path to your financial freedom. Ignoring business basics could send you to the poorhouse, but respecting them could leave you rolling in cash.

EASY STEP 4

---●---

The Blueprint:

A 5 Point Business Plan

"Good plans shape good decisions. That's why good planning helps to make elusive dreams come true."

—Geoffrey Fisher

Chapter 17

Blueprint Point 1: Get a PIG

I can't believe it—you're still skeptical! That's okay. As I said before, acknowledge your fear and take a step forward. Right now, you're likely asking yourself, "To buy or not to buy?" It's a hard decision. You're afraid of losing money that it took you forever to save up. I've personally dealt with all these unanswered questions and daunting doubts that are racing through your mind. So put your mind at ease by methodically answering these questions in a business plan, your roadmap to success. The problem is that most people don't make one at all, or they wait until they're already in financial trouble to start looking for a plan.

Don't get me wrong—I hate writing business plans. They are a lot of work, but when I'm done with one, I'm really happy I put in the necessary time to create it. I won't walk you through a full-blown comprehensive plan here. The Small Business Administration (SBA) has a great tool at http://www.sba.gov you can use to create your own comprehensive plan. However, whether you're evaluating an investment property or contemplating starting a business, you must consider five key points before doing so. These points form the foundation of your business plan. I will say it again: real estate investing is a business and should be treated as such. And for any business to be successful, there must be a plan. These points can be used to create a simple plan for real estate or for any other financial venture you're considering. It's a "quick and dirty" method to help you evaluate whether you should pursue the venture. As elsewhere in the book, in this discussion, I'll continue to use real estate as the basis for your venture.

The first point in the five-point business plan is to get a PIG. To differentiate a real PIG from a failed venture or a harebrained idea masquerading as a PIG, complete the following steps:

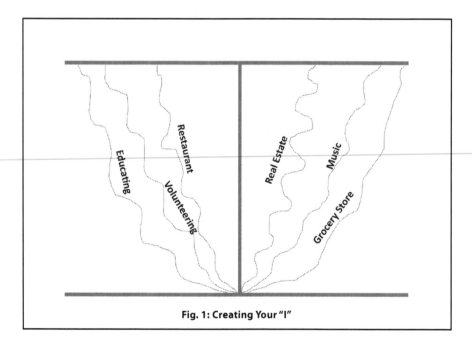

Fig. 1: Creating Your "I"

1. Pick a PIG from your "I." (See Life Assignment #6)
2. Use lead-generator sources to source the PIG..
3. Run your PIG through the Rule of 3: Asset Litmus Test.
4. Acquire or create the PIG.

Picking your PIG should be easy thanks to the previous Life Assignments that helped you identify what you are most passionate about. Remember, this passion will keep you focused and moving forward when you hit bumps in the road. And believe me, you will definitely experience ups and downs. Review your "I" and pick a PIG:

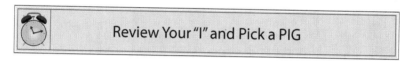

Review Your "I" and Pick a PIG

Now that you've chosen the kind of business you would like to build, it's time to find or to build that business. How do you do that? Regardless of whether you choose to create a new business or to acquire an existing one, lead-generator sources in your "I" industry will be your primary means for finding or creating potential PIGs. Common lead-generator sources include the following:

- Internet search engines
- Business brokers
- Real-estate agents
- Attorneys and CPAs
- Newspaper classified ads
- People in your personal network(s)
- Investment clubs and associations related to your type of business

For this example, you've chosen real estate as the business you wish to build, and one of the best sources of leads for your business type is a real-estate agent. You've selected an agent to be a member of your team—later I'll discuss how to qualify members of your team—and have been presented with the following scenario:

> *Your real-estate agent just called to say he's found an amazing three-bedroom/two-bath house in an okay neighborhood. He estimates that it will take about $5,000 in cosmetic repairs and fewer than thirty days to get the house fixed up and rented. After rehab, the rental market rate is $1,200 per month, and the house is a foreclosure with an asking price of $85,000, although you can probably get it for $80,000 if you can close quickly. Is this a PIG?*

You can answer this question very easily by running your PIG through the Rule of 3: Asset Litmus Test. The agent has sent over the listing information, and you've passed it along to your mortgage broker, who has then provided the pertinent information needed to complete your test. Here are the results:

Example 1: Real Estate PIG Asset Test

Scenario: Your real-estate agent just called you to say he's found you an amazing 3 bedroom/2 bath house in an okay neighborhood. He estimates that it will take about $5,000 in cosmetic repairs and fewer than 30 days to get the house fixed up and rented. After rehab rental market rate is $1,200 per month, and the house is a foreclosure with an asking price of $85,000 although you can probably get it for $80,000 if you can close quickly. Is this a PIG?

Rule #1: Positive Cash Flow: Your Mortgage Broker says you will need 20% Down Payment and 3% Closing Cost. Your total monthly mortgage payment for a 30-year fix rate investment loan on $64,000 at 5.75% is $374. You do so more due diligence and find out that the annual real estate taxes are $800 and the hazard insurance is $600.

Income		Expenses	
Gross Rental	$1,200	Mortgage Payment	$374
Total Income	$1,200	Real Estate Taxes	$67
		Hazard Insurance	$50
		10% Vacancy/Repair Reserve	$120
		Total Expenses	$611

Monthly Cash Flow = Total Income − Total Expenses
= $1,200 - $611
= **$589**

Asset Test #1: Does this *PIG* create a positive monthly cash flow?
(**X**) Yes or ( ) No

Rule #2: Cash-on-Cash Return on Investment (ROI): Here is the total cash you'll need to take out of your savings account that currently pays you 1.5% yield:

$16,000 - 20% Down Payment
$1,920 - 3% Closing Cost
$5,000 - Rehab Cost

—Continue on page 98

—*Continued from page 97*

$3,666 - Reserves (6 mos. of Total Expenses)

$26,586 - Total Cash Investment

Cash-on-Cash ROI = (Monthly Cash Flow *12) / Total Cash Investment
   = ($589 * 12) / $25,586
   = $7,068 / $25,586
   = **27.6 %**

Asset Test #2: Is the Cash-on-Cash ROI **(27.6%)** > Current Rate of Return **(1.5%)** ? (X) Yes or (   ) No

Rule #3: Appreciation Rate
(**X**) Yes or (   ) No – You did some calling around and found that the local government just declared the area a revitalization zone and has a 5-year plan already underway to develop the area. Home prices are expected to double.

It's a PIG if you have 3 YES's !!!

Drum roll please . . . you've found a PIG! The question now is: should you really buy it? All you're really doing here is outlining the steps to help you decide whether the property you're evaluating is a great investment. And to be honest, a great investment is any investment that meets the particular investing criteria that you have defined. For example, I will never suggest that your investment *must* have a minimum 15 percent rate of return or that the property you buy should have an expected annual appreciation rate of at least 25 percent. These types of hard-line rules would be absurd, as each person begins his or her real-estate-investment career in a different financial situation and in varying markets. This book provides criteria to guide you as you begin investing, but your own personal experiences will refine and add to the criteria described in these pages. Each deal will bring with it a new experience and a different set of rules to add to your analysis arsenal.

Recall that while I was overanalyzing an investment, another investor scooped it out from under me. I quickly learned the meaning behind the proverb *"the early bird catches the worm."* Thus, I've developed this litmus test to let you quickly evaluate each point and help you make a fast decision regarding whether the venture you are considering is right for you.

Put on your overalls, boots, and straw hat, as you're ready to be a farmer and acquire your first PIG. The best farmers are those whose PIGs are real assets. Remember, an asset is simply something that puts money into your pocket. Before you protest that you don't have any assets, just wait—you certainly do, if you'll take the time to create them. Each business identified in your "I" is an asset. Because real estate is the type of business I'm using to illustrate these techniques, the asset you will create in this example is a residential real-estate investment firm. This firm will buy and hold real property, so you'll need to start by acquiring property to fund your asset. I'll spend a great deal of time later discussing how to identify potential properties and acquire them, but right now I want to point out a basic principle.

A key attribute of any successful business owner is to be able to effectively leverage OPM and OPT. Both of these are precious resources. When considering the acquisition of your asset, think about the practical details of how you will do so. Unlike buying CDs, stocks, bonds, or mutual funds, it's often fairly easy to secure capital to purchase real estate. Banks understand real estate and will readily lend you money to buy it as opposed to other investment vehicles. Regardless of the state of the economy, banks are still in the lending business. Lending is how banks generate revenue. The guidelines may change on how you get approved but the money is still there. And the best thing about real estate is that if conventional means of obtaining a mortgage from a bank don't work out, you can be as creative as you want with your financing, depending on what you and the seller agree upon.

While working with beginning investors who come to my monthly cash-flow group meeting, I've found this issue to be the top reason why they haven't invested: they don't know how to secure financing for a deal. Financing is the last thing I worry about when selecting an investment, as I know I can employ OPM concepts to get my deals done. What I'm more concerned about is finding a great deal. If you find a great deal, you can find the financing, but the deal has to make sense. Thus, doing a quick-and-dirty analysis should help you ascertain whether the potential investment is a great deal; if so, simply submit your offer. In fact, part of this great-deal analysis can be done during the due-diligence process, which I'll discuss shortly; right now, the focus is on submitting your offer. *"He who has control has power."* So get your property under contract and deal with the other fine points later.

I want to ensure that you accomplish this objective of acquiring an asset. At the risk of being repetitive, let me reiterate (because it really is a simple yet critical point to learn): an asset is anything that puts cash into your pocket, and a liability is anything that takes money out of your pocket. For example, while living in a hot real-estate market like New York City, I've heard novice investors say, *"Well, although I'll be paying $1,000 per month out of pocket to help cover what I don't get in rent, my investment property will* *be worth a whole lot more in five years.*" According to my litmus test, this property does not fall under the asset category, although to some investors it may appear to. This property takes $1,000 per month out of the investor's pocket, and the investor is gambling that future interest rates and other market conditions will be favorable enough to increase the property's value, thus allowing the investor to recoup all the money he lost during the holding period before selling. I'm not a fan of playing "Texas Hold 'Em" with my money, so gambling on appreciation does not pass my Asset Litmus Test.

Where is this investor in today's down market cycle? Probably in foreclosure or in financial ruins, robbing Peter to pay Paul in an effort to stay afloat. The real-estate market took a nosedive that no one expected, and now banks are stuck with an unimaginable number of foreclosures they don't know what to do with. Have no fear—one man's trash is another man's treasure. If you choose real estate as your business type, I want you to build your firm, but you need to do so in the right way. I remember once going to a foreclosure auction in the Bronx. Almost a year later, I was at another auction for that exact same property. Some foolish investor purchased that property at the first auction without doing the proper homework and ended up in foreclosure.

What about "flippers," you may ask? Well, you're only as good as your last flip, which means flipping properties is a job—and that definition certainly throws this investment technique out of my asset test. I repeat: *It's a job.* That Bronx property I mentioned was purchased as a potential flip right before the market crash.

Now that you are comfortable with your own investment criteria, go back to your starting question: "To buy or not to buy?" Before you jump the gun and give that final "yes," you must consider one last thing: due diligence. In the earlier example, your real-estate agent only provided the sales listing, and based on that information and a few phone calls, your initial investigation said that this property was a good deal. The Asset Litmus Test indicated that the property was a good investment, but you need to make sure it's not a future failed venture in disguise. Due diligence is the process by which you delve deeper into researching the physical and financial aspects of an asset. Whether it's a piece of property or a business, do not start this process until you have the asset under contract to purchase. Typically, you'll have an agreed-upon time between signing the contract and actually closing escrow. This time is your due-diligence phase. The escape clauses in your sales contract is your way to legally get out of the deal if the due-diligence is not favorable.

First review the physical attributes of your asset. Here are some of the things you'll definitely want to consider:

1. **Inspection**—One of the first things you want to do is get the property inspected. Hire a trained professional to perform the property inspection. They perform thorough investigations of all the mechanical systems and other aspects of the house, including the roof, plumbing, electrical wiring, and heating and air conditioning, to make sure all the systems are in good working order. They also look for hidden health hazards, such as mold, and some may even warn you of the presence of lead-based paint. You need to be aware of all the existing problems and potential problems with a house before buying it. Based on the results of the inspection, decide whether to move forward with purchasing the property. A deal breaker would be any repair that costs more than you are willing to invest in time and/or money.

2. **Location**—I'm sure you've heard the phrase "location, location, location," especially when it comes to real estate. Make sure that your property is located in a desirable neighborhood that's going to attract good renters. Your real-estate agent can provide demographic information for the property's zip code. In determining location, consider the following five characteristics that are favorable conditions likely to attract renters:

   2.1. Gender—"Papa was a rolling stone," as the famed song lyric goes, and you certainly don't want "Papa" rolling through your complex. Based on my personal experience and that of colleagues, you'll find in the rental market that women tend to be more stable than men. This trait may be because of the current state of the American family household, in which it's not unusual for a single mother to be raising one or two kids. Thus, you'll want to pick a property that's located in an area that includes more women than men.

   2.2. Age—Young whippersnappers are moving out of their parents' houses, getting their first cars, and going to or finishing college, ready to take on the world. They tend to move around a couple of times and maybe even between a few different cities before they settle down. Thus, you'll want a property in an area where the median age is under thirty-five. Typically, around the age of thirty-five is when people are settled into their careers and thinking about starting families if they haven't already done so. They're ready to stop being renters and to purchase their own homes, so look for younger people to be your potential tenants. This personal experience is backed up by a study from the Joint Center for Housing Studies of Harvard University that states that four out of every ten renters are under the age of 35.

2.3. Income—Why would you buy a house where people couldn't afford to pay the rent? Doing so is the quickest way to find yourself in the poorhouse. Again, your objective here is to make money and not lose it, so make sure the rent is affordable in that neighborhood by evaluating it against the area's median income. If the rent exceeds 38 percent of the median income, then you definitely have to reevaluate the deal. Your agent said that the after-rehab market rent of the house was $1,200 per month. Suppose the area's median income is $40,000 per year, making the affordability threshold $1,267 per month (38 percent of $40,000 divided by 12). Because the projected rent is less than the threshold, this property is affordable for the average person currently living in the area.

2.4. Population—You'll want to buy properties in areas that have population influx. The area's demographic information typically includes historical information, so look at the population to make sure it has been trending upward and not downward. A decrease in the population means people have been moving out of the area, which means fewer renter prospects for your property.

2.5. Crime Statistics—I vowed to never be a slum landlord. As part of my commitment, I make sure that the places where my tenants live are safe and clean. My motto: *"I wouldn't rent it if I wouldn't live in it."* Thus, you'll want to make sure that the area is safe. A quick call to the local police precinct could inform you about criminal activity in the area. Also, demographic information is available online listing criminal activity by zip code and by neighborhood as well.

3. **Amenities**—What do renters want? A great leasing agent knows exactly what people in that neighborhood are looking for. Perhaps they want ceiling fans, a dishwasher, wall-to-wall carpeting, fresh paint, central air-conditioning, free parking, proximity to public transportation and a good school system, a washer/dryer connection, new renovations, and so forth. Find out what renter prospects are looking for in this area by asking a leasing agent, and try to include as many amenities as possible in your property. Factor in whatever items are necessary as part of your renovations budget. In my experience, you should always paint the rooms and clean the carpets as a bare minimum when getting a house ready to lease. Having the right amenities helps you demand the highest rent in the area and helps you lease the property quickly.

Now review the financial attributes of your asset. Here are some of the things you'll definitely want to consider:

1. Market Value—The agent told you that the property had an asking price of $85,000 and that you could probably get it for $80,000. You made an offer of $80,000, and the seller accepted it. However, how do you know that the house is worth $80,000? You certainly don't want to overpay for the property. Price is the point where the seller and the buyer agree upon the value of a good or service being exchanged. Here, the price was set at $80,000 during the negotiating phase of the deal, but what do you or the seller know? Licensed professionals who do not have any financial interest in the property (unlike you and the seller) can provide an unbiased opinion regarding the property's worth. An appraiser will do area research and a physical evaluation of the asset to tell you what it's actually worth in the current market. The results of the appraisal report will help you decide whether to move forward with purchasing the property. I certainly wouldn't purchase a property paying more than the appraised value.

2. Financing—Never let money stop you from acquiring an asset. If you truly have a great deal, you'll find the money. Look for the cheapest money with the best terms. Several different sources of financing are available, but here are the three most common types that I've used:

> **a. Conventional Loans**—These are conforming and nonconforming loans from banks, credit unions, and other financial institutions. Loan limits change every year, but as of this writing, a conforming loan is any loan amount under

$725,750, and nonconforming loans are higher amounts. Because a loan is like a hot potato for a bank, it typically sells your loan on the secondary market to replenish its cash supply so it has money to lend to the next applicant. Because these loans are packaged and sold on the market as mortgage-backed securities, all these loans typically follow the same lending guidelines. Thus, it doesn't make too much sense to shop around for the best interest rate for a loan, because banks get their money from the same money-supply source—the bond market. Instead, make sure that the mortgage broker you're using is fast and an expert at maneuvering the lending guidelines. Getting a nonconforming loan may require more shopping around, as each lender creates its own lending criteria for these higher-limit loans. Remember, the financing only works for your deal if the monthly payment generates positive cash flow as part of the litmus test.

b. **Government Loans**—Government loans are administered by lending institutions backed by the government in case you default on the loan. They include FHA, VA, and SBA loans. When all else fails, you usually can qualify for a government loan. However, be ready for extensive paperwork to be provided, as the government requires every "i" to be dotted and "t" to be crossed. Because exotic mortgage-backed securities sent the housing market into a downfall, regulatory measures have since tightened on all types of financing.

c. **Private Loans**—Examples include loans from friends and family, hard-money lenders, seller financing, and personal or business unsecured credit lines sourced to your deal as private loans. They are not regulated like conventional and government loans. They typically carry higher interest rates and unfavorable terms, but they are the easiest type for you to get. One site I use to find hard-money lenders is http://www.scotsmanguide.com. Hard-money lenders are more concerned with the value of the asset and the equity as opposed to the lending worthiness of the borrower (income, assets, and credit).

Regardless of the type of loan you find, don't let its interest rate kill your deal. In my seminars, I often ask this question of novice investors: "*Is an interest rate of 24 percent too high to pay?*" Oftentimes I get a quick response of "yes." However, suppose that you structure a 100 percent financed deal with a 24 percent interest rate that passes the Asset Litmus Test. Then I would say, "*No, this interest rate is not too high.*" If it's the best rate you can find for your deal and it still passes the test, I say do the deal, especially because you'll have to put no money of your own into it. I love these types of deals.

On the topic of interest rates, how do lenders typically determine your rate? They are driven by risk-based pricing. The more likely it appears that you may default on the loan, the higher your interest rate will be. Your income, credit, and assets are the three basic criteria used to qualify you for financing. Your income or income produced from the asset tells the lender your "ability to repay the debt." Your credit represents your historical payment pattern and management of capital. Your score tells the lender your "willingness to repay the debt." Based on statistical models, a score of 680 or higher means you're less likely to default on your loan. Your assets are the cash (savings, stocks, bonds, mutual funds, etc) you have available if a lender requires any down payment and closing cost to acquire the property.

Sometimes to acquire the best financing, you may have to take on a partner. Maybe you are short of funds for a down payment and closing costs and need a "money partner." Maybe your credit score is not very high and you have to take on a "credit partner." I try to take on as few partners as possible to avoid a "too many cooks in the kitchen" nightmare. However, if you must take on a partner to get the deal done, do so. As with any other type of negotiation, you'll have to negotiate with this person an agreement that defines the terms of your partnership. Have this information in writing before you close on the deal so each partner's role and financial reward are spelled out upfront. This will lessen the chances of a future lawsuit between you and your partner(s). In one particular deal, the lender said I didn't have enough experience working in that type of business, so I had to take on a "management partner" to get approved for the loan. I take on management/operational partners (examples of OPT) in every deal, a strategy I'll discuss later in the business plan.

3. **Renovations Cost**—Get a couple of contractors to look at the property and give you a quote for how much it will cost to make any necessary repairs and upgrades. I suggest getting at least three different quotes, but beware: the projects will always take more money and more time than estimated. I've never heard of a contractor finishing before deadline and under

budget. Cost overruns always occur, so be safe and add 20 percent to your budget to cover these things. When selecting a contractor for the job, don't let a low price be the ultimate deciding factor. You get what you pay for, so check the contractors' references to see how they did on past jobs. Quality work done up front will save you from higher repair costs later.

4. **Operating Cost**—All your assets will have some associated operating costs. For a rental house, they usually include real-estate tax, insurance, common utilities, and property management cost. Validate for yourself the property's current operating expenses. I never assume that what the agent or owner may tell me is accurate. I request a copy of the current annual real-estate tax. I also call the county tax assessor's office to see if it can provide the estimated taxes for the following year. Some areas have extremely high taxes, and a huge increase the year after you've purchased the property could send you into a negative cash-flow position, so you definitely want to have a short conversation with the assessor. Also get a quote for hazard insurance. You have the option of insuring the house just to cover the financing or for the entire value of the property. I suggest covering the entire value. Ask the insurance company whether the property is located in a flood zone. Again, you don't want any surprises occurring right after you purchase the property, and acquiring flood insurance later could be expensive. Finally, if you are going to hire a property management company to handle the day-to-day operations of your property, you'll definitely want to evaluate a few

and make your selection during this due-diligence phase. They usually charge between 7-10% of the gross rent but can save you a great deal of time and aid in the process of finding excellent tenants.

5. **Preleasing**—I cannot overemphasize how important this step is. I truly expect to be in a positive cash-flow position on the day of closing. Thus, to make this happen, I use my due-diligence period to market the property and to find a tenant. You can typically negotiate anywhere from thirty to sixty days to close on a property. You, your leasing agent, or your property management company should get a tenant into contract subject to your actually closing on the property, of course. An added bonus of doing the preleasing during this phase is that the tenant can be involved in the renovation process. For example, the tenant may make special color requests for paint or carpet, thus getting that person exactly the rental he or she wants. And you have a signed lease and security deposit in hand on the day of closing, putting your mind at ease because you know you'll have the rental income to carry the property. Don't forget that you tested the rental market rate the agent provided, so right before closing, you should know exactly how much rent you can get for the house. Now, all that's required is for your contractor to quickly finish the renovations so your tenant can move in on time. Not preleasing means you are not in a positive cash-flow situation on the day of closing, and who knows how long it could take for you to find a qualified tenant? Until you do, you're paying out of pocket to cover the monthly expenses.

Now that you've found a PIG, analyzed it, and performed your due diligence, it's time to close. This is the final step, and the easiest. You just sign a bunch of documents, and then you get the keys to the property. You'll feel as though you're signing away your first born, but don't worry—you've taken the necessary precautions to make sure you're getting a good deal.

See how well you understand the concepts discussed here by testing your knowledge on a potential business. A business broker has sent you this listing for a bakery you may want to buy:

Bakery For Sale

Priced to sell. All offers considered. Bakery located in downtown business district. Asking price is just $200,000. Long time staple in the neighborhood. Cash cow.
Call 555-5555 for more information.

Fig. 4: Bakery Classified Ad

Write Down Your Questions about the Bakery Ad

Read the classified ad a few times, carefully. Each time you read the ad, as questions pop into your mind, write them down so you can compare them to the questions I had when I read the ad.

Here are some of the questions that popped into my mind when I read this ad:

1. *What is the seller's motivation?* Essential to successful contract negotiations, you must know the seller's motivation. Did you notice some buzzwords in the ad, such as "priced to sell," "all offers considered," and "cash cow"? They almost make it sound too good to be true. Remember, the asset can exist in one of three states: negative cash flow, break-even, or positive cash flow. If the seller is losing money, these buzzwords are meant to distract you from discovering all the physical or financial problems with the business. The seller just wants to dump this bakery, fast. If the business is honestly a cash cow, the seller could just be ready to retire and needs a quick sale or needs cash to acquire another asset. For example, I found a great eight-unit apartment building in Spanish Harlem, New York. The owner had held the property for more than twenty years, but he was ready to retire to the Caribbean. That plan was his motivation, and he was willing to be as creative as I wanted to be on the financing, because the sooner he could sell his building, the sooner he could start his retirement. Thus, some ads that seem too good to be true actually are true, but you won't know either way until you do a little more research.

2. *How long has the bakery been for sale?* Many things get better with time, and that's certainly true when something is for sale. That is, they get better for you, the buyer, but not for the seller. The longer an asset sits for sale on the open market, the more negotiating power you have over the price. For example, say that a property has been on the market for more than 180 days. Don't laugh—that's very common in the current housing crisis. The longer that property sits for sale, especially if it's vacant, the more motivated the owner becomes to sell it. And that desperation leads to deep discounting on the price the owner is willing to accept for the property. Imagine you've been trying to sell your vacant property for 180 days. That means you've been making mortgage, tax, and insurance payments on that property for six months. It also creates other hazardous conditions, because vacant properties often fall prey to vandalism and squatters. I've found that the key to creating a win-win in negotiations is to put myself in the other person's shoes and to imagine the current financial situation that he or she is in and the related emotions being experienced. If it's a distressed situation, tapping into those emotions and using them to your advantage will get you the best deal. Don't feel guilty about using this information to your advantage—although you're getting a great deal on this distressed property, you're also helping the seller find an answer to his or her financial problem, creating a win for you as the buyer and a win for the seller.

3. *What "value plays" can I make?* If the bakery is a "cash cow," what value plays can I make to improve it? You never want to purchase an asset just to maintain its current status quo condition. You should also evaluate the asset's current income stream and operating expenses to uncover areas for improvement that will increase the overall value of the asset. This is a value play. The bakery ad states that it's in the business district and is a staple of the community. A staple means it's been around for a long time, and if the original owner is still operating the bakery, he or she might not have grown with the times, especially when it comes to technology. You may look at the current operations and see some opportunities to increase the income using modern technology. For example, you could create a Web site that allows online ordering with local delivery, and you could implement social networking that rewards customers who follow your Facebook, Twitter, and FourSquare accounts. You want the current customer base to become champions for you and to promote your bakery. These acts could all increase the income stream. You may also notice that the current owner doesn't do a great job of controlling inventory. Tweaking some techniques will decrease your cost of goods sold. Other small changes may include replacing the lighting with energy-efficient lightbulbs and installing a water-conservation kit for the customer restroom.

I could go on and on with a list of questions and hypothetical situations created just by reading the ad. All these questions will get answered during the contract negotiations and due-diligence process. Remember, the early bird catches the worm, so you don't want to get bogged down in all these semantics just yet. For now, contact the broker and ask for the financial statements so you can run the bakery through the Asset Litmus Test. If it passes the test based on the initial financials provided, enter a purchasing contract and then start your due-diligence process. Secure your financing and close on the deal to become the new owner of a bakery.

Chapter 18

Blueprint Point 2 : Hide Your PIG

*M*any people out there would love to have your PIG on their dinner tables. They are professional thieves who prey on farmers who don't protect their PIGs. After evaluating and acquiring the asset, you must secure it. The United States is a very litigious society. Lawsuits run rampant throughout the court system. Even if no reasonable doubt clouds your claims of innocence, the time and money spent to endure a frivolous lawsuit are not worth it. For example, a patron claiming an injury that resulted from slipping and falling in the bakery could be detrimental to the owner's personal assets if the proper legal protection is not in place.

The flipside is that this same court system allows business owners to protect themselves. You don't have to be completely vulnerable to the money-hungry vultures out there. Different legal entities provide levels of asset protection. The most common entities are sole proprietorships, C corporations, S corporations, general partnerships (GP), limited liability partnerships (LLP), and limited liability corporations (LLC). Garrett Sutton, Esq., a *Rich Dad* adviser, has a book called *Own Your Own Corporation* that provides explanations of these entities and which is right for your business. Specific legal and tax ramifications are associated with each type. Michael Lechter, Esq., another *Rich Dad* adviser, has a book called *Protecting Your #1 Asset* that talks about protecting intellectual property.

For now, I'll discuss a limited liability corporation (LLC). Legal experts advise that this entity provides the greatest level of asset protection for real-estate investors. Other forms of protection are also available, such as a land trust, an irrevocable living trust, or a combination of all three. An LLC is a type of hybrid legal entity that allows business owners to have the limited liability features of a corporation as well as the tax benefits. It helps you protect your personal assets. Some of the benefits of forming an LLC include the following:

- It's one of the easiest and least-expensive forms of incorporation.
- The owner has limited personal liability for business debts.
- Allocation of profits or losses does not need to be proportional to the ownership interest.
- It does not pose a double taxation threat, because the LLC is not a separate taxable entity but instead flows through to the individual owner's tax returns.

Most banks will not allow you to purchase residential property in the name of your LLC. Residential property is generally defined as a cooperative, a condominium, or a one- to four-family dwelling. Although your personal name is on the mortgage with the bank, you may be able to hold the deed or ownership interest of the property in the name of your LLC. This is where asset protection comes into play. If your lender will not allow you to own the property in the name of your LLC, you may consider employing a quitclaim deed to transfer the ownership of the property out of your personal name and into the name of your LLC. This way, the rental lease is between your LLC and the tenant, rent payments are made payable to your LLC, and all other related real-estate documents are in the name of your LLC. This gives you some level of asset protection from liabilities or lawsuits that might result from your real-estate-investment activities. If you form and manage the LLC correctly and such claims arise, then generally only the assets owned by the LLC can be named in that claim.

Here are the steps to get your business up and running:

1. **Form a Corporation**—Most states allow you to form a corporation online. Just perform an Internet search for your state followed by "division of corporation" (for example, "New York Division of Corporation"). The instructions are typically easy to follow and allow you to form your own corporation within a matter of minutes. The only critical point I want to make here is that every state requires you to have a physical address in that state for the sake of registered agents. A registered agent is the person or place where legal documents can be served in case a lawsuit should arise.

2. **Establish a Business Address, Phone Number, Fax Number, and E-mail Address**—I like to keep my business life

and personal life separate, so I never put my home address on anything. Even if you're running a home-based business, I suggest using an alternate address, such as a post office box. You should also set up a separate phone line and business e-mail address. For both of these, I use Google's Voice and Gmail features.

3. **Get a Tax ID Number**—The government recognizes businesses just as it does real people; citizens have Social Security numbers, and businesses have tax ID numbers. Go to http://www.IRS.gov to search for instructions for how to obtain an Employee Tax Identification Number (EIN). Just as you formed a corporation online, you can apply online for your EIN. The instructions are easy to follow and yield your ID number within minutes.

4. **Open a Business Bank Account**—You must open a business banking account. Otherwise, you'll comingle your personal funds with your business funds, which is called "piercing the corporate veil." Mixing funds negates all the hard work you put into creating your corporation for asset protection. Many banks offer free business checking accounts and require low minimum deposits (say, $25) to open them. They generally only require a copy of your incorporation papers and a photo ID to get started. What I love about these accounts is that oftentimes the bank will offer you an application for a business credit card right on the spot. And typically if you have good credit, the bank may start you with a $10,000 unsecured credit card/line, no questions asked. This situation is great,

because it gives you access to $10,000 to help you finance your business. If you're going to have a lot of employees, I suggest picking a bank that offers an online payroll system and QuickBooks integration, the accounting software you'll most likely use when managing your business. If you're going to accept credit cards, ask the bank about its merchant accounts. For the one house you're purchasing in this book's example, you would only need a business checking account and a business credit card.

5. **Cyberspace Your Business**—If you're not online, you're not in business. In fact, cyberspace is one of the first places where an underwriter looks for information about you and your business as part of the financing approval process. Many Web site hosting companies offer free or very inexpensive plans that allow you to create a homepage for your business. You also have the luxury of establishing a social networking presence for your business; I suggest making a Facebook page and setting up a Twitter account for your business, at a minimum.

6. **Establish Your Business Credit**—Generally, you must be in business for at least two years to really start applying for high amounts of credit. However, some merchants, such as Home Depot and Lowes, will often give you business credit even if you're a newly formed corporation. I suggest getting one of these types of accounts for your real estate PIG, as you can use it to help manage your cash flow by charging equipment and supplies needed to maintain your

properties. In addition, although many banks will offer you a credit card or small credit line when you open a business account, you should also register your business with Dun & Bradstreet (DNB). DNB is to business credit as TransUnion, Equifax, and Experian are to personal credit. Some underwriters check this company for information about you as well when approving your business for financing. Simply registering your new business on its Web site is all you need to do for now.

7. **Document Your Business**—Create stationery and business cards for your business. The lease and other documents you'll need for your real-estate business should display your corporation name. Again, do not create documents with your personal name, because you'll open yourself up to personal liability for the business. Although you'll sign all the documents for your business, you'll do so as an officer of the corporation and not as you the individual. Any previous documents generated in your personal name, such as the property deed, need to be transferred to your business name.

Although these are some of the basic steps for getting your business running, I recommend consulting with a real-estate attorney and CPA who specialized in tax strategies for your business type when creating your asset protection plan. The most common form of asset protection for real estate is an LLC, but you'll want these types of people on your team of advisers to tell you precisely what kind of corporation to form for your business.

Chapter 19

Blueprint Point 3: Manage Your PIG

Any investment has to be managed if you expect to achieve the desired results. Real-estate management can range from day-to-day management of rental income to proper record keeping of wholesale transactions. Regardless of which facet of real estate investing you decide to pursue, you'll need to implement some sound management principles to ensure the success of your business.

In my real-estate cash-flow technique, management is the key component to a successful deal. The buy and hold transaction incurs monthly income and operating expenses. The income and expenses must be managed correctly to provide the maximum amount of passive income that the property can realize. I'll talk in more detail later about property management. For now, know that the key lies in increasing your income while at the same time decreasing your expenses.

The key to management is building a successful team. I'll discuss what I call "The Winner's Circle" later in the book. In real-estate management, several layers are needed to create a proper system of checks and balances within the business.

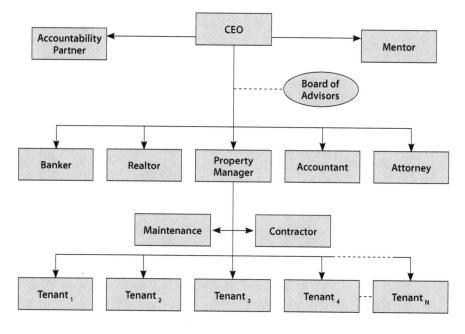

Fig. 5: Management Team

The first layer includes an "accountability partner." This is a person who is neither a Good Crab nor a Bad Crab, because he or she doesn't have an opinion about your business or about you. This person is simply a sounding board for your ideas and helps you keep track of your commitments. It's preferable for your accountability partner to be working on building or growing a business as well so you can provide an even exchange of support.

My accountability partner is my CPA. Though ours is a professional relationship, I have grown to love and to respect her. She's come to know my personality and is great at identifying the areas where I need help, such as organizing my ideas so they are manageable or getting off my butt instead of procrastinating. I work with her on the same issues as well. It's impossible to meet physically, because we live in different cities, but we have established a weekly conference call lasting no more than ten minutes in which we discuss how each of us is progressing. During this brief call, we review which task items we committed to and completed the previous week. We review what needs to be completed this week and any new items that need to be added to the task list. We provide emotional support for each other by encouraging one another to stay focused on the tasks at hand. We will occasionally send an inspiring one- or two-line e-mail message between calls to make sure we're doing what we're supposed to do.

Again, she is a partner with no judgments. Now don't get me wrong—we are both entrepreneurs and occasionally offer each other opinions and guidance on something, but for the most part, the calls just provide the emotional support that a business person needs to get through the week.

The first layer also includes a mentor. I've found that successful people love to talk about what they do. They live in the world of abundance, not scarcity, so they don't mind sharing information. Why not learn from someone else's mistakes so you don't repeat them? Isn't this what your parents tried to teach you as you were growing up? For example, a young child sees a pot of boiling water on the stove. His mom tells him not to touch the pot, as it will burn his hand. The mom is speaking from experience, as she's been burned before while touching a hot pot. She only wants to protect her son from making the same mistake. Your mentor will keep you away from those boiling pots out there. And trust me, no matter what business you're in, you'll always face problems, and it's great to have someone experienced to help you come up with solutions to them.

How do you find a mentor? Start by looking in your community. Try to find someone who is successfully running a business just like or very similar to the one you're looking to start. Visit the person and ask if he or she is interested in being your mentor. Be respectful of the person's time and only meet monthly, quarterly, or just occasionally. I try to pick my mentor's brain over lunch. Business people are often busy, but everyone stops at some point to eat. Have a set of questions already prepared that you need help with. Your mentor will be very instrumental in your reducing your learning curve to make your business successful. I've asked fellow successful business owners but was met with opposition to being my mentor. I quickly found out they weren't as successful as I thought they appeared to be. I should have known, as successful people live in the world of abundance and not scarcity. The opposition was a result of them feeling threatened by me as a new competitor in their market space. They failed to see that each business niche creates its own unique market and there is room for all of us to be successful. I remember I had asked a business owner if I could meet with her for advice on opening up my restaurant and she only agreed to do so if I paid her for her time. I was a little taken back by her response as she had recently gone out of business. I wanted her advice of what not to do in starting my new business. After I thought about her response, I quickly ascertained why she had not been successful in her own venture.

The next layer is your board of advisers. The board of advisers is just like the board of directors for your corporation, except they don't get compensated. They are a group of people who help you govern your company. Because they are not compensated and sit on your board purely on a volunteer basis, you will often find straight shooters who tell you what you *need* to hear and not what you *want* to hear to operate your business. Because they are not paid, you need to be respectful of their free time and hold meetings to review the progress of your business at convenient times. Types of people you may want on your board include an attorney, a CPA, and an operations manager. Remember, successful people love to talk about what they've done and offer their opinion to others. Use this to your advantage.

You may or may not need a board of advisers right away. As your business grows and problems grow with it, you will have the option of adding this board. That's why it's denoted with a dotted line on the management chart. Trust me, you'll know when the timing's right to add such a board.

The next layer is the operations layer. This layer includes individuals who have skill sets and expertise in areas that you don't (or don't have time to work in) that are required to run the day-to-day operations of your business. For your real estate PIG, you would need a property manager, an accountant, an attorney, a real-estate agent, and a banker. The roles of all these professionals are as follows:

1. **Property Manager**—This person can make or break your business. He or she is really the top person who controls the daily operations of your properties. The property manager should have experience in managing the type of properties that are in your portfolio. People in this profession may work on commission or on a salaried basis. They also find and hire the staff you need to keep the property running, such as maintenance technicians and contractors. The maintenance technician fixes the things that get broken in the property.

The contractor makes major property improvements, and because you'll always be looking to expand your portfolio of properties, having this contractor on your team will also be useful in making the initial improvements necessary upon purchasing new properties. A good property manager will fulfill many duties, which I'll cover in more detail in your ninety-day Action Plan.

2. **Accountant (CPA)**—Your accountant keeps you out of trouble with the IRS. The real-estate business can be very lucrative, but with the wrong accountant on your team, it can turn into a nightmare. One of the key benefits of owning real estate is its tax advantages, so you certainly want to make sure you have a very competent CPA on your team. Believe it or not, I've seen accountants at investment-club meetings trying to solicit new clients when they themselves don't own property. How can they effectively advise someone on issues they haven't experienced themselves? I suggest finding a CPA who has investment property in his or her portfolio. This person should be familiar with the tax loopholes you can use to reduce your tax burden.

3. **Attorney**—Like your CPA, your attorney should hold investment property in his or her portfolio. (In fact, holding property should be a requirement for all the people who are in the operations layer of your management structure.) Your attorney should have a close working relationship with your accountant, as they must collaborate to come up with one strategic plan for you that will provide the

best asset protection while maximizing the tax benefits of owning real estate. If your property manager prefers not to handle tenant evictions, your attorney will be the next option (but an expensive one) to process any evictions that may be required. He or she should be well versed in the landlord-tenant laws affecting your property.

4. **Real-Estate Agent**—This person is a key team member who is constantly looking for properties that fit your investment criteria. He or she may also assist in the leasing processing. This person is licensed and works on commission. In fact, I pay my agents premium commissions. I've found that doing so makes them work harder at finding me the best properties, because if they keep me happy as an active investor, I'll continue to close on properties that earn them commission checks. Money talks, and it certainly keeps my agents motivated to find me great deals.

5. **Banker**—Your banker will advise you on financing options to acquire your deals. Bankers are bankers by and large, but I advise you to find a banker with experience in working with real-estate investors. The underwriting guidelines for investment property are much more stringent than owner-occupied properties, so you need an experienced banker on your team. Your banker should also be able to work with investors who use creative financing techniques. Finding a really good banker has been a difficult process for me. They are not versed in creative financing techniques so I've had to retrain their thinking to get my deals done.

The last and final (but best) layer is the tenants. They are the source of your cash flow. I never like to let the tenants know I'm the property owner, especially in the larger apartment building in my portfolio. During my property visits, I like to ask questions that are indirect but give me information on how well the property manager and maintenance people are working. If the tenant knows I'm the owner, he or she may not feel free to candidly be my eyes and ears. I formally communicate with my residents via newsletter, and I create an open-door policy by providing them with an e-mail address or voice-mail service where they can communicate problems, questions, and concerns.

My resident relationship is reciprocal: the money doesn't flow one way. I also give back during special celebrations, such as Valentine's Day, Thanksgiving, and Christmas. Small gifts to each resident during these times let them know that I care. It's important to show appreciation to your residents to reward them being great tenants. I also try to sponsor a summer picnic or outing for them. Thus, as part of my cash-flow analysis, I allot money for a "community fund" where I set aside a portion of the gross rent to strengthen the sense of community among the residents.

All these layers of management will definitely be instrumental in your running a successful real estate PIG. You should begin the interview process of team members even before acquiring your first property. Knowing who to go to for questions as you go through the process will prove to be very beneficial. Start to build your team sooner rather than later, and then use your team to grow your assets. As your portfolio grows, so will your team of experts.

Chapter 20

The Winner's Circle

Every successful business owner knows how to manage resources. Resources harness the leveraging power to grow the business. The most valuable resources are OPM and OPT. You must invest one or both of these. Nothing in life is free. Even in "no money down" real-estate deals, you may not be investing your own money, but you're certainly investing your time to find motivated sellers who fit your investment strategy. Regardless of the resource you decide to invest, they should be managed effectively.

OPM could be from the bank, your friends, family members, or other investors. OPT comes from those people who contribute their time to be part of your team. It's impossible to be everywhere and to do everything. You cannot put 110 percent of your efforts toward a goal. Entrepreneurs are constantly creating new ideas, techniques, businesses, and so forth. Being innovative is an inherent part of their nature. I know you're an entrepreneur, or you wouldn't have had the tenacity to make it this far into this book.

But because many entrepreneurs create ideas faster than they can implement them, they really function as visionaries. A visionary is a person who literally fantasizes with enthusiasm but with very little consideration as to what is actually possible or feasible. An entrepreneur is able to take that vision, recognize opportunity, and organize available resources to bring that vision to life. The entrepreneur definitely sees the benefits of managing resources and building a team.

The Adizes PAEI framework is a great model to use to build an effective team. It helps define people, their roles, and the relationships between them. The Adizes model understands that no individual can possibly effectively manage all the demands of a corporation. However, the business is sure to fail if it falls victim to the cliché "too many chiefs and not enough Indians," meaning too many people are deciding what to do and not enough people are doing the work. The PAEI framework defines the Producer, Administrator, Entrepreneur, and Integrator as the four most-effective types of people to include on your team.

Dr. Ichak Adizes's book *How to Solve the Mismanagement Crisis* describes these conflicting roles and styles. For an organization to be successful in the short and in the long term, it must properly develop all four functions. The Producer is charged with the task of producing results for the organization. While the Producer focuses on what has to be done, the Administrator focuses on the details of how to do it. Handling all the activities and functions directed at planning, organizing, scheduling is the Administrator's role. Meanwhile, the Entrepreneur continuously monitors the environment and makes the necessary changes to create new opportunities or to respond to threats to ensure that the organization remains successful. And finally, the Integrator strives to develop an organic consciousness in the organization by affirming core values and establishing a shared sense of purpose. This role focuses on developing a cohesive team that will make the organization more efficient over the long term. Each role and its effect on the organization are summarized in the chart below:

Role	Focus	Organizational Effect	Effective Timeframe
P – Producer	What?	Functional	Short term
A – Administrator	How?	Systematic	Short term
E – Entrepreneur	Why?	Proactive	Long term
I – Integrator	Who?	Organic	Long term

http://www.thecompletelawyer.com/volume1/issue1/article.php?artid=7

Most novice real-estate investors start out using OPM. This idea is what usually captivates their attention in the first place. The notions planted by those late-night infomercials that claim you can become a millionaire overnight doing "no money down" real-estate deals are quite convincing. Ponder for a moment the amount of money you've likely spent on seminars and home-study courses. Believe me, I've been a victim of the hype as well and have had no problem using my credit card to join the late-night infomercial feeding frenzy. Be that as it may, one behavior eventually led to another. I found myself with so many courses and sources of information that I was in overload. I would start one of these courses and try to use its touted techniques, but my unfocused behavior kept me in a vicious cycle of starting and not finishing an idea before moving on to the next. How could I effectively accomplish anything? All my efforts were never focused on one venture, as I had too many projects pulling my resources in different directions. It took a while, but I finally determined the behavior I needed to change. I call this concept *"The Winner's Circle."*

I can't tell you how often I think of some new idea for a business, a new process I want to implement, or a method to improve a current one. But they're just ideas, and without a Producer on my team, they remain just ideas. I've found that my excitement comes from thinking up the idea, but after that it's all downhill. I find very little pleasure in implementing the idea, although I love to see the end result. I owe it all to my short attention span. I'm surprised that I've even been able to focus long enough to write this book. But I have, and that's because I learned about Adizes's framework, which brought me to this concept of the Winner's Circle. I realized that I had all these ideas floating around in my head. I even went so far as to make them New Year's resolutions to add to my "to do" list. I would find myself incrementally working on each idea, and each idea would incrementally progress along the path of actually becoming a reality. Look at the figure below. Look at the figure on page 135.

I found myself not in a Winner's Circle, but a Loser's Circle. Bringing an idea to life went from taking two to three months to two to three *years*, and even then most ideas hadn't seen the light of day. My other work also seemed to be in vain, because I would work on one idea for a short period of time and then switch to

<u>Winner's Circle</u>

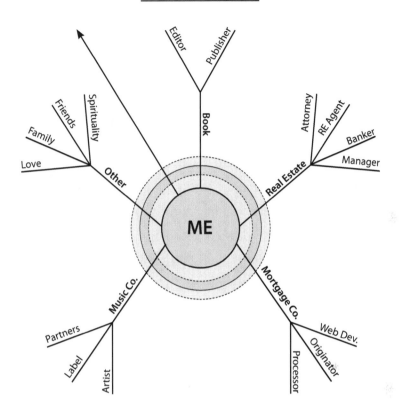

another idea, and then yet another. I realized that I wasn't getting anywhere financially, and I felt emotionally drained and physically tired. Being unfocused consumed and wasted my most precious resource: time. I vowed to never fall victim to a PDA or to a planner on my desk, but time management really is the key to success. I had to become more efficient.

It wasn't easy, but I learned to organize and to prioritize my ideas to be successful. I assigned weights to each item according to how realistic the idea was and the amount of time it required. This ranking system allowed me to focus on my goals more clearly, starting with idea number one. It wasn't until I focused that I realized I really couldn't do it all. I needed "Mini Me's" to serve as carbon copies or extensions of myself. Taking the time to focus and to stop working on each idea simultaneously allowed me to build my team. For example, when I began to focus on my real-estate company, I quickly realized that I needed the talents, experience, and advice of my real-estate agent, attorney, accountant, mortgage broker, and property manager on my team in order to build a successful business. I needed these Producers, Administrators, and Integrators to bring my ideas to life. I must admit that it took some time to find the team members who were the right fit for my company, but once I did, I quickly realized the importance of this Winner's Circle. The people I pulled into my circle of influence were there to guide me through the business decisions I made. Relinquishing the notion that "I can do it all" or "I can do it for less" not only allowed my idea to become a reality faster than I could imagine, but it also yielded an emotional revelation: I finally felt that I had actually accomplished something. And the weight of that idea was lifted off my shoulders once it became a reality. Being the Visionary/Entrepreneur that I am, my other ideas didn't completely fall by the wayside, but they had to wait their turn in my hierarchy of realism. I'm still working on that "Other" arm that extends from "ME" in the diagram, the arm in which I have grouped the other important aspects of my life, such as love, family, friends, and spirituality. Once I learn how to incorporate them into my financial career, I will have truly mastered my Winner's

Circle. And when I do, you can read all about it. It is yet another living work in progress, *The Balancing Act.*

If you're anything like me, when you notice an area for improvement in your life, you probably go on the defensive. I can hear the chatter running through your head now: "No, that's not me. I'm very organized and focused. I'm just not where I want to be financially because I don't have the time." Well, stop now and complete Life Assignment #10, "Winner's Circle." Grab a piece of paper and a pencil, and draw your own Winner's Circle. Draw a different arm for each type of activity that consumes your time during the week. I think you'll be surprised when you realize how many different directions your time is being pulled in.

Life Assignment #10: Winner's Circle

Think about all the things you have going on in your life. Sit down, prioritize them, and decide which ones you can and are willing to work on first. If buying a property isn't your first priority, that's fine. You'll be more effective when it *is* your first priority. In the meantime, this idea will sit and wait its turn. So I don't suggest starting your Action Plan (which I'll discuss later) until you've figured out what's in your Winner's Circle. When buying a property is your top focus, that's the time to start your plan.

The more information you gain, the better equipped you will be to manage your asset. A lot of information is available, and quite a bit of it is free. One way to gather information is through networking. The more people you meet who know what business you're in, the better off you are. Nine times out of ten, they will know someone who can use your product or service or will connect you to someone who can help you grow your business. Look online to find groups where you can meet potential customers, vendors, and business associates. I have joined groups through http://www.Meetup.com, my local chamber of commerce, real-estate-investment clubs, landlord associations, and so forth. Having all these people in my network is an added benefit to me and to my business.

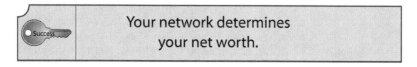

Your network determines your net worth.

As you grow your network and your team, figure out what type of person each is as defined by the Adizes PAEI framework. Knowing each person's strengths and weaknesses will help you better utilize them on your team and successfully manage them as a crucial resource. One team member's strength should offset another member's weakness. Your team is as strong as its weakest link.

Chapter 21

Blueprint Point 4: Leveraging Your PIG

Leveraging is one of the greatest tools you can use to create multiple income streams. It's important to use leverage wisely when creating each strand of your "I." Leveraging your current assets to acquire more assets is one way to amass a lot of wealth in a short period of time. I'll explain the "equity stripping" technique as it applies to real estate investing, because that's how I built my financial empire.

Real estate really lends itself to this concept. If you're not following this method, you're letting your "sleeping giant" actually *sleep,* and money that's lying dormant in the form of appreciated equity isn't making you any money at all. You're merely working hard for your money as opposed to making your money work hard for you. Novice investors get entrenched in the idea of being equity rich and cash poor, but effective leveraging of this equity allows you to buy more positive cash-flow properties, thus increasing your passive income. Remember, the goal of your "I" is to have many PIGs working hard for you so eventually your passive income will

How fast does your money work for you?

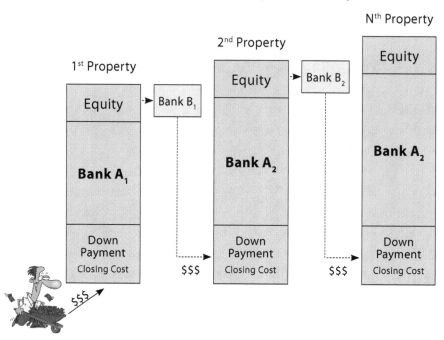

Exhibit 1: Velocity of Money

surpass your monthly living expenses. Then, you will be financially free. Ask yourself how hard and how fast your money is working for you. What are you doing to leverage your current assets and investment accounts? Put your PIGs to work.

The way you awaken this "sleeping giant" is by refinancing your property using an equity line of credit or another OPM concept. Suppose you used your savings for the down payment and closing costs to purchase a single-family home for a purchase price of $100,000 (Property 1). You put down $10,000 as a down payment and took out a mortgage for $90,000. The property has since appreciated at a rate of at least 7 percent per annum since the time of purchase. Assuming the market continues to grow, within three years of implementing your buy and hold strategy, that property contains $33,500 worth of equity:

Market Value	$122,500
Mortgage Balance	$88,000
Total Equity	$33,500

Note: I've taken into account principal pay down on a fully amortized thirty-year 6 percent fixed-rate mortgage. So after three years, you've accumulated $33,000 of wealth. The best thing about this money is that you didn't have to work for it. It's like *free* money that just grew from your passive income stream. This property passed the asset litmus test.

Most banks will allow you to borrow up to 90 percent of the equity in your property. Thus, from Property 1, you could open an equity line of credit for about $30,000. This home-equity line of credit can be used for many purposes, such as renovating the property, taking a vacation, consolidating debt, buying a car, and so forth—you don't have to disclose the use of the equity line to the bank. Home-equity lines offer several benefits, such as quick approval, because it's an equity line and not a refinanced transaction; access to your credit line through use of a checkbook and/or credit card; and possible tax advantages for the interest you pay on the equity line.

You could also use this $30,000 to acquire another asset. The money covered the down payment and closing costs to acquire Property 2. This time, your leveraging technique afforded you the opportunity to buy a single-family home for $250,000. Your down payment was $25,000, and you took out a mortgage for $225,000. Using the same appreciation assumptions from Property 1, within one year, this property would have $44,500 in equity:

Market Value	$267,500
Mortgage Balance	$223,000
Total Equity	$44,500

This $40,000 could now be used to acquire another asset, and this is how you build your portfolio, starting with Property 1 to Property N^{th}, as displayed in Exhibit 1: Velocity of Money. As you acquire assets with a positive cash flow using the Asset Litmus Test, you will build equity that gives you leveraging power to use later. In this example, within four years, you would have increased your passive income through the rental properties' positive cash flow while at the same time increasing your net worth by $44,000.

The appreciation rate of your property and how quickly you tap into the equity determines the velocity of your money. The faster you continue to leverage the equity of your current assets to buy more appreciating assets, the faster you'll increase your passive income and grow your net worth. Again, the goal is not to be equity rich and cash poor but to leverage correctly and wisely.

Wait just a second! I've demonstrated the "equity-stripping" technique without explaining how to incorporate the Asset Litmus Test. Look at the figure, below. Using the leveraging technique, you would have acquired a total of fifteen units in your portfolio, generating a monthly positive cash flow of $5,877. You started with only $10,000 from your savings, but that initial investment has been leveraged into $1.1-million in properties while increasing your net worth and monthly cash flow.

I won't go into details explaining the additional expenses that come with certain unit types, but I do want to point out that investing in commercial property is far easier than residential, and you

How much monthly cash flow would you have from the 4 properties?

	Property 1	Property 2	Property 3	Property 4	Totals
Property Type	1-unit	2-unit	4-unit	8-unit	15 units
Leveraging Power	$ -	$30,000	$40,000	$50,000	$120,000
Purchase Price	$100,000	$250,000	$300,000	$450,000	$1,100,000
Down Payment + Closing	$10,000	$25,000	$30,000	$45,000	$110,000
Bank A Mortgage	$90,000	$225,000	$270,000	$405,000	$990,000
Bank B Mortgage	$ -	$30,000	$40,000	$50,000	$120,000
Income					
Gross Rental Income	$1,200	$2,600	$5,200	$9,600	$18,600
5% Vacancy Reserve	$(60)	$(130)	$(260)	$(480)	$(930)
Laundry Income	$ -	$ -	$ -	$120	$120
Other Fee income	$ -	$ -	$5	$20	$25
Total Effective Income	**$1,140**	**$2,470**	**$4,940**	**$9,120**	**$17,670**
Expenses					
Management Fee	$120	$260	$520	$960	$1,860
Repairs & Maintenance	$21	$42	$83	$167	$313
5% Repair Reserve	$60	$130	$260	$480	$930
Mortgage Payments					
Bank A	$540	$1,349	$1,619	$2,428	$5,936
Bank B	$ -	$111	$148	$185	$444
Real Estate Taxes	$33	$83	$100	$150	$367
Insurance Payments					
Private Mortgage	$131	$328	$394	$ -	$853
Hazard	$23	$56	$68	$101	$248
Flood	$ -	$ -	$ -	$50	$50
Common Utilities					
Water/Sewer	$ -	$ -	$ -	$150	$150
Gas	$ -	$ -	$ -	$60	$60
Electric	$ -	$ -	$ -	$ -	$ -
Trash	$ -	$ -	$ -	$90	$90

—*Continue on page 146*

—Continued from page 145

Pest Control	$8	$17	$33	$67	$125
Landscaping	$13	$22	$38	$72	$145
Advertising/Marketing	$ -	$ -	$ -	$100	$100
Legal	$ -	$ -	$10	$10	$20
Supplies	$ -	$ -	$ -	$25	$25
Accounting	$12	$12	$12	$12	$48
Community Fund	$2	$4	$8	$17	$31
Total Operating Expenses	**$963**	**$2,414**	**$3,293**	**$5,123**	**$11,793**
Monthly Cash Flow	**$177**	**$56**	**$1,647**	**$3,997**	**$5,877**

Note: All of our 1st mortgages are at 6% on 30-yr fix rates and our home equity line of credits are at PRIME + 1% or 4.50% interest only payments. Properties appreciate at 7% per annun.

get the extra benefit of economies of scale when managing your expenses. As shown in the figure, leveraging allowed you to acquire a one-unit property, then a two-unit, then a four-unit, and then you decided to take the leap to commercial properties and purchase an eight-unit property. And all this only took four iterations of the stripping technique. I love these PIGs.

Any business you create and grow can be leveraged. In this real-estate example, I talked about equity lines, but financing is available for any profit or nonprofit business that you create. The most common form of bank financing for a business is a Small Business Administration (SBA) loan, which is administered by the U.S. government. These loans originate through private-sector lenders who receive repayment guarantees from the SBA. They are typically loans to small businesses that are unable to secure financing under reasonable terms through normal lending channels. I've applied for and used SBA funding to start a business. It's a great program, and you can find out more about it by visiting http://www.SBA.gov. Small businesses help spur the U.S. economy's growth, and I'm glad to have the SBA on my side.

Another form of leveraging your assets is using unsecured financing. I talked briefly about this concept earlier. Credit-card companies love to provide financing to small businesses. Once you create your asset, especially if you've registered as a business entity with the government, you'll probably start receiving offers in the mail for business credit cards. They can be used just like regular credit cards, except approval is based on you and your business, and they should be used for business expenditures only. I've used unsecured business credit cards to get access to cash for down payments and closing costs to acquire most of my PIGs.

You may also decide to seek private financing by selling shares of your corporation represented by the appreciated equity of your asset; you may take out a loan from a private lender; or you may take on a new partner in your company, exchanging equity for a cash injection into your business.

Chapter 22

Blueprint Point 5: Bye-Bye, PIG

Every successful business plan has an exit strategy. This is the point where you decide to get out of your business by liquidating its assets. In the buy and hold real-estate strategy, that point may be when your property has achieved a certain appreciation rate or you have exhausted all the tax benefits, such as phantom depreciation. Or maybe you're simply ready to play a bigger game by moving on to a different type of investment strategy, such as trading up from single-family to commercial properties.

Knowing when to get out is one of the keys to successfully running your business. Deciding when that point is and the strategy applied will vary for each person and their current circumstances. However, lets look at some different reasons that could motivate you to sell:

1. You're no longer passionate about the business.

2. The market has reached its peak or has started to take a downturn and you think that now is the time you can command the highest sales price for your business.

3. The management structure in place is no longer working and you can't find the right managers to turn the business around.

4. Your accountant has told you that you've held the business so long in your portfolio as an asset that there are no more tax advantages to keeping it in your portfolio. For example, in real estate the two greatest tax advantages are being able to deduct the mortgage interest paid on financing for the property and the phantom depreciation expense. The depreciation schedule is 27.5 years for residential (1-4 unit properties, coops, and/or condos) property and 39 years for commercial property. After this time period, you no longer have the depreciation expense tax benefit, so it may be a good time to sell the property.

5. Other conditions in the environment have changed that lead you to believe you should sell. For example, the neighborhood where your property is located has increased criminal activity or new competitors for your bakery business have entered the marketplace and the competition is fierce.

No matter what your motivation is for why you want to sell your business, as a savvy investor, you will constantly monitor your business to know when is the right time to get out. You'll work with a real estate agent or business broker to sell your asset. They possess the expertise to evaluate your asset and tell you the best price they think the market will offer. This is a great time to start getting financial documents together that the prospective buyer might ask for, such as the current Profit & Loss Statement, the past 2 years of tax returns, current rent roll if it's real estate, current list of vendors, contractors, and suppliers who have contracts with you for services provided, etc. Your selling broker will let you know exactly what documents you should have prepared for the prospective buyer's due diligence. It's best to start early, as it could take some time to gather all the documentation.

Several prospective buyers will evaluate the physical and financial condition of your business and make you an offer. With the assistance of your team members (Seller representative, CPA, Attorney, Management, etc) you'll evaluate if this is a good offer and whether to sell the business to the Buyer.

When you sell your business, there may be capital gains taxes to pay. This varies with each business type, how long you held the asset in your portfolio, your acquisition cost and how much you sold it for, your current tax bracket, etc. To lessen the impact of the capital gains tax on your income you can do what's called a "1031 Exchange" if you're selling real estate. Consult with your CPA about this process and if it's something you should do when selling your business.

The five-point business plan is by no means a comprehensive business plan. It's simply a quick checklist you can use to analyze your investments. But when you buy your business, it's not too early to contemplate an exit strategy and when and why you might want to get out.

Chapter 23

Win-Win Formula

Having your cake and eating it too...now that's what I call life. How would you like to buy real estate at such a deeply discounted price that you walk into the deal with equity, enjoy positive cash flow while you own it, and use it as leveraging power to buy more assets? That's just what I did, and I call that my Win-Win Formula.

Win-Win? Yes, you read the name correctly, and before I explain this magical formula further, I'll address your number-one fear up front: What if the deal goes bad? So what if it does? What is the one thing you can always do with real estate? *Sell it!* That's always a realistic option. Someone is always willing to buy your property, although the price will vary. This resale value is something you'll have considered when performing your due diligence before purchasing the property.

The Win-Win Formula combines the five-point business plan with the Rule of 3. It involves purchasing real estate with some level of assurance of turning a profit. The Win-Win Formula really requires overcoming the fear of success, not the fear of failure. The tools that I have provided in this book are simply that: tools. But if you don't put these tools to use, then you've already failed. In reality, you have nothing to lose and all the knowledge, experience, and wealth in the world to gain—you deserve to be a winner.

> ## Taking the first leap of faith makes you successful!

You've earned the right to be successful. You were born ready for success. How do I know this? You've already overcome the biggest challenge in your investment career: you've decided that you want more out of life. Otherwise, you wouldn't be reading this book to learn how to create more wealth. I challenge you to keep learning by reading other books on investing so you can increase your financial literacy.

Now that I've determined that you're already a winner in the real-estate-investment game, I'll dedicate the rest of this book to showing you how to stay in the game and to never return to the sidelines as a mere spectator, watching everyone else play and have fun with your money. Just follow the ninety-day Action Plan to get started.

EASY STEP

90-Day Action Plan

"When was the last time you woke up and realized that today could be the best day of your life? Participate in your dreams today. There are unlimited opportunities available with this new day. Take action on those wonderful dreams you've had in your mind for so long. Remember, success is something you experience when you act accordingly. Success is not something you HAVE, it's something you DO."

—*Steve Maraboli*

FREE Bonus

Register now at http://www.CEOeBooks for your
FREE Bonus. Get the useful tools and resources every
successful entrepreneur shouldn't be without.

The goal over the next ninety days is to get your business up and running. You've done a lot of the heavy lifting already by completing your Life Assignments, but now I'll get into the finer details of what you need to do to be on your way to financial freedom. Your commitment to the next twelve weeks will change your life!

— Transformation Week #1 —

~

Getting Your House in Order

This week you'll clean up the mental and physical clutter so you can be in a place to create the you who's passionate about life and what you do.

(✔)	Action Task	Tools
	Creed—This is your commitment to your financial future. Let it be a constant daily reminder of your focus. Pull out your creed and post it somewhere you will see it every day, such as the bathroom mirror, the refrigerator door, or the back of your front door.	• Life Assignment #7
	Resignation Letter—Place your resignation letter in a hidden place in your current workspace. Soon you will be giving it to your employer as you move on to be in business for yourself.	• Life Assignment #9
	Crab List—Review and update your Crab List. Take this task very seriously. It will probably be emotionally draining to remove yourself from people who are not positive influences in your life, but you *must* do it.	• Life Assignment #1 • Strong will

Credit Report—Get a copy of your credit report. I suggest a tri-merge report from Experian, TransUnion, and Equifax. If your middle credit score is below 680, work on credit repair to get it increased quickly.	• AnnualCreditReport.com • Experian.com, TransUnion.com, or Equifax.com
Financial Statements—It's time to face the facts. Don't feel bad, as most people live off credit and have negative monthly cash flows, but by completing the statements honestly, you'll know where you are and where you need to go. The Income Statement, Balance Sheet, Working Money, and Cost of Capital worksheets will provide great insight: • Look at which living expenses you can decrease or eliminate. • Review your rates of return on all your investments to see where you can move money around to provide a better return. • Call up creditors and try to get your interest rates lowered, your credit lines increased, and your current balances transferred.	• Bank, 401(k), stocks, and Investment-account statements • Credit-card and loan statements • Strong negotiating skills
Create Your "I"—Now that some time has passed since you initially created your "I," review and update the living expenses and passive income. This is the cornerstone of the new financial empire you're building. It's a great idea to post a copy of it next to your creed.	• Life Assignment #6 • Financial Statements
Home Office Space—Set aside a designated area in your home as office space so you can begin to organize as you build your business.	

~

Pick a PIG

Over the next two weeks, you'll focus on building a strong team. Your management team is the backbone of your organization, and a weak foundation leads to a weak company. So start off with the right people, but don't be afraid to change them out as necessary. You'll also start to evaluate current assets you can purchase and grow or assets you can build from scratch. As part of this process, you'll start to create your comprehensive business plan.

(✔)	Action Task	Tools
	Pick a PIG—Review your "I" and pick the business you're the most passionate about right now in your life.	• Life Assignment #6
	Accountability Partner—Start building your management team. Review your "Good Crab" list and call up a few people. Explain to them what their roles would be as your partners and how they can benefit from being your partners, as it's a reciprocal relationship. Once you've found a partner, schedule your first ten-minute call to get your partner up to speed on what you accomplished during Week #1 and what you need to get accomplished before the next call.	• Fig. 5: Management Team • Life Assignment #1 • Telephone/E-mail
	Mentor—Remember how vast your network is. Look for someone who is successful in the industry of the business you selected to create from your "I." Preferably this person should not just work in the industry but be a business owner him- or herself. Set up your first luncheon. This first meeting will be you listening to the mentor talk about his or her experiences and asking what advice he or she could provide to you a new entrepreneur in the same business. If no one is currently in your network, search on the Internet for clubs, associations, and organizations in your industry that you could look to for finding a mentor.	• Fig. 5: Management Team • Life Assignment #1 • Internet • Telephone/E-mail

Other Team Members—One of the twenty-three billionaire principles that I learned at a Bill Bartmann seminar is that "copying is better than innovating." Regardless of the business you've chosen, someone else is probably already doing it. Look for sample business plans and actual similar companies on the Internet. See what kind of people are on their management teams and think about the skills and expertise you will need on your team. Start looking for people who fit the criteria and begin inviting them to join your team.	• Fig. 5: Management Team • Internet • Telephone/E-mail
Form Your Corporation—Decide which legal entity will provide you with the best asset protection plan and tax benefits. Pick a name for your business and form the corporation. Try not to use such words as "Funding," "Development," and "Investor" in the title, because they could prevent you from getting unsecured business lines. Set up your mailing address, phone number, fax number, and e-mail address for your business. Apply for an IRS EIN and open a business checking account.	• Attorney and CPA • Post Office • Vistaprint.com • Google Voice and Gmail • IRS.gov • Local bank
Business Plan—Start working on your business plan using this online SBA resource: http://www.sba.gov/content/online-courses-starting-your-business (click on "How to Prepare a Business Plan)	• SBA.gov
Follow Up—Continue working on any uncompleted task, such as credit repair and getting your home office set up.	• Various

~

Find a PIG

Over the next three weeks, you'll start evaluating some PIGs to purchase or getting data you can use to forecast income and expenses of a start-up PIG you're creating.

(✔)	Action Task	Tools
	Find a PIG—Start contacting brokers (real estate, business, investment, and so forth) and ask to have listings e-mailed or faxed to you. You can also look in newspaper classified ads and listings from Internet searches. Run each PIG through the Asset Litmus Test.	• Telephone/E-mail • Classified ads • Internet searches • Life Assignment #11
	Financing Sources—If you have good/excellent credit, apply for some business unsecured credit cards/lines. Review your 401(k)/retirement statements to see if you have any funds to borrow against or to withdraw to start your business. Start creating a list of private lenders, such as friends and family members, in case you need additional funding. Also do searches for hard-money lenders. Start building a list of potential credit, money, and management partners you can call on to help you close your deal.	• Online applications • Internet searches • "Working Money" worksheet Network of people
	Accountability Partner—Make weekly progress reports.	• Telephone/E-mail
	Mentor—Provide a first-month progress report and seek advice.	• Telephone/E-mail or luncheon
	Business Plan—Continue working on your business plan using the SBA online resource: http://www.sba.gov/content/online-courses-starting-your-business (click on "How to Prepare a Business Plan)	• SBA.gov
	Follow up—Continue working on any uncompleted task, such as forming your corporation and repairing your credit.	• Various

~

Get a PIG

You've spent the previous three weeks diligently viewing properties or reviewing business financials, and now it's time to go to contract on your first PIG.

(✔)	Action Task	Tools
	Sign the Contract—A few properties you've evaluated have passed the Asset Litmus Test. Which one do you pick? Go with your gut instinct. Review the one you choose with your mentor and other members of your team. Get your team to help you negotiate the price with the seller or define your start-up cost if you're building a business from scratch. By now, you should have an attorney on your team to draw up the contract. All that's left for you to do is to sign it.	• Telephone/E-mail • Life Assignment #11 • Management team • Strong negotiation skills
	Due Diligence—It's time to get into the bones of the deal, dotting every "i" and crossing every "t." Check and double check your numbers. Every income and expense item needs to be investigated. If you can get historical data, do so; never accept anybody else's word for the accuracy of the numbers provided to you, especially that of the seller or the broker.	• Telephone/E-mail • Copies of leases, contracts, bank statements, financial statements, utility bills, and so forth
	Apply for Financing—Apply for financing with your banker, who will also guide you by requesting certain documentation and reports as part of the financing due diligence. Obtain an appraisal of the asset (property or business) and hire a professional to perform a physical inspection of the asset.	• Banker • Appraiser • Inspector • List of financing sources

Preclosing Items—Start advertising and marketing your opening. If your business is real estate, start looking for a tenant. If it's a retail or service business, communicate to the potential customers you identified in your business plan that you will soon be open for business. If your business needs employees, start the interview process.	• Local papers • Online ads • Agencies and organizations that could be customer-lead sources	
Accountability Partner—Make weekly progress reports.	• Telephone/E-mail	
Mentor—Provide a second-month progress report and seek advice.	• Telephone/E-mail or luncheon	
Business Plan—Continue working on your business plan using the SBA online resource: http://www.sba.gov/content/online-courses-starting-your-business (click on "How to Prepare a Business Plan)	• SBA.gov	
Follow Up—Continue working on any uncompleted task, such as finding alternative financing sources, refining your management team, and repairing your credit.	• Various	

— Transformation Weeks #9, #10, #11 & #12 —

~

You're a Proud PIG Owner!

This is the moment you and your team have been working so hard for. It's time to close your deal and get dirty while getting your PIG open for business.

(✔)	Action Task	Tools
	Close the Deal—Can you believe it? The moment has finally arrived. It's time for you to actually acquire your PIG. Closing Day is such a wonderful feeling of accomplishment. Make sure you celebrate your success!	• Telephone/E-mail • Management team • Celebration party
	Construction/Renovation—If any renovations need to be done to your real estate, you now have the keys and can start the process. If you need to turn utilities on in your business name, now is the time to do so.	• Management team • Utility applications
	Initial Inventory/Supplies—Order any initial inventory and supplies you need for your business.	• Suppliers and vendors
	Training—If you've hired any employees, get them trained and ready for opening day.	• Management team
	Opening Day—This is the day your tenant moves into your property or your first customer walks though the door, and it's a great feeling. Take some pictures to keep as inspiration to acquire the next asset.	• Management team • Customer • Camera
	Resignation Letter—Depending on the size of the deal you've just done, update your financial statements so you can see where you stand. You may be able to hand your boss your resignation letter and say, "take this job and shove it."	• Life Assignment #9

Accountability Partner—Make weekly progress reports.	•	Telephone/E-mail
Mentor—Provide a third-month progress report and seek advice.	•	Telephone/E-mail or luncheon
Business Plan—Continue working on your business plan using the SBA online resource: http://www.sba.gov/category/navigation-structure/ starting-managing-business/starting-business/ writing-business-plan	•	SBA.gov
Follow up—Continue working on any uncompleted task, such as due diligence, refining your management team, and preclosing items.	•	Various

Congratulations, you're in business.

Continue to update your business plan and grow the PIG!

Some Final Words

I hope you've enjoyed reading this book as much as I've enjoyed writing it. But, even more, I hope that you've started to put these principles into practice. You've been given a lot of information, and a plan that can lead you towards financial freedom. Remember what I said earlier in the book, no one can do this alone. Seek out like-minded people with similar goals so that you can support and help one another along this exciting and liberating journey. Build your team.

Feel free to join my cash-flow club in New York City, or seek out a similar group where you live. Remember to just say yes! This isn't some crazy scheme I dreamed up. It has worked for me, and for many others. I'm including some testimonials in Appendix A for you to read through to inspire you with more real-life stories of how it worked for others.

May success be yours in all that you do.

Appendix A

Testimonials

"In the business world, everyone is paid in two coins: cash and experience. Take the experience first; the cash will come later."

—Harold S. Geneen

Introduction

What you are about to read are real testimonials from real members of our RichDadNYC Cashflow group (http://www.richdadnyc.com) that I founded and is currently the leader of in Harlem, NY. These testimonials reflect each member's unique experience of being a part of this group and under my leadership. The "5 Easy Steps To Financial Freedom" were born out of this group and are a reflection of my experience as the leader inspiring and empowering individuals along their quest.

Read each testimonial and understand that each member was once like you. The difference is that they took action. They made a conscious decision to pursue financial freedom in their life. If they can do it, then you can do it too. Store these experiences in your heart and mind, and remember them when you are unsure of whether to continue along your fun and amazing journey to financial freedom.

Testimonial 1: Quit Your Day Job

After graduating college, I did not land a job conducive to my education and had no choice but to move back home with my mom. I happened to obtain a job as a worker in a newspaper factory making $8.00 an hour. I had student loans and past-due credit cards that I couldn't afford to pay. I was afraid to answer the phone because I didn't know how to tell a bill collector that I couldn't pay. My credit and financial situations were going downhill.

My mom had heard of a book called Rich Dad, Poor Dad and

suggested that I read it. After taking her advice, I felt my financial paradigm shift. I read many books like it and was determined to be a real estate investor and business owner. Six months later, I obtained a job with the government in New York City as a supervisor. The pay was decent, but the job didn't offer the financial freedom I was yearning for. A friend from church who attended Duane's Rich Dad group in NYC recommended that I join. I took her advice and started attending in October of 2009.

During my first meeting with Duane, he told me something that I will never forget, "My goal for you is to quit your day job." I quickly agreed and have been pursuing that goal ever since. Within two meetings, I knew I belonged there. Soon after, I decided to implement what I was learning.

I posted the creed, "If I do not buy a cashflowing property by December 31, 2010, I ought to be ashamed of myself," on my bedroom wall. This creed was a constant reminder for me to take action and avoid excuses.

Duane mentioned that there are companies who can repair your credit. He also taught me that it is better to have control over an asset than to own it—"He who has control has power." With this in mind, I hired a company to repair my credit, and began to sublease the rooms in a 3-bedroom apartment I was renting. I contracted with an agency who sent me international students to host. They paid me $700 per room per student. I was paying $850/mo. to rent the apartment from the landlord. Within two months, I was making an extra $1,000 per month, which I used to pay off my bad consumer debt and student loans.

With my credit restored, I was able to qualify for a mortgage.

I closed on my first property on March 31, 2010. As of today, I am cashflowing about $600 per month in addition to living rent-free. With the creed still on my wall, I decided to scratch out "first" cashflowing property and write "second" cashflowing property by December 31, 2010. On December 7, 2010. I closed on my second property. Currently, I am cashflowing $165/mo. off this property.

Now I am working towards purchasing my third investment property, and I'm creating two businesses. Without the principles and advice I obtained from the Duane's RichDad group, I would not be where I am today. I know that if I continue to attend the monthly meetings, I will reach my goal of retiring before I am 30 years old.

Testimonial 2: Get Your Financial House in Order

I joined the cashflow club, because I had purchased a coop in 2002 and then a condo in 2005 and didn't know the first thing about real estate or what I should be doing with both properties. So I went on a quest to find like-minded people who could give me some much-needed advice and support.

I joined the group in 2007, right before the crash of 2008. Duane would say every month, "People get your Financial House in order, because cash will be king." I soon realized what a blessing this information was to my life. I began to pay closer attention to my budget, I started to track my finances and decrease expenses. I now understood that I was in the rat race and the only way to get out was to become financially free.

I am currently working on turning my passions into a business.

I am developing a Children's App and writing a book about all the things I have learned in the process of maintaining and selling my properties.

I found during this process that fears are very real and can slow your process or stop it totally if you do not daily remind yourself of who you are and what you want! That's why joining a group of like-minded people is very important. It's a resource of encouragement for those who need a boost and an energizer for those who are on the path.

For those out there thinking of starting your own business, you must know yourself and your skill set before you begin. If you love food and want to open a restaurant, you don't need to know how to cook or have worked in the restaurant business before. It helps, but it should not be the thing that stops you. What you need to know is that any skills you are lacking can be covered by partnering with an expert in that field, someone who has the skills and knowledge you'll need to make your business a success.

Testimonial 3: Just Over Broke

I joined the RichDadNYC group because I wanted to be interconnected with a group of like-minded people and learn about financial freedom. Since joining the group, I learned about long term and short term goal setting, managing my finances & learning to leverage other peoples' money to acquire wealth. My personal passion that I turned into a business was remodeling and decorating. I truly enjoy purchasing foreclosed homes and having them reformed and rehabbed into a better, enhanced state.

It was difficult for me to believe in myself and get over the hurdle of fear, to learn enough about the business and get into the game. I have not yet resigned from my day job, but I have reduced my time to 21 hours a week and my passive income from my real estate investment currently exceeds my earned income as I own several rental properties.

I had no passive income before I started investing. I only had earned income, which allowed me to pay my bills each month without a problem while working like a dog and always feeling tired. I had no time for myself and felt that there had to be a better way than this never-ending cycle of working for earned income. My philosophy is that a JOB will have you **J**ust **O**ver **B**roke. A job will never afford you the true financial freedom that comes with being an investor or business owner. As a last piece of advice, always remember that time and money are your two most precious resources.

Testimonial 4: Reborn

I was feeling unfulfilled in my life as a whole. I had a great girlfriend (who is currently my wife), a great family to come home to everyday, good friends to hang out with, but I was stuck at a job that I didn't enjoy. As happy as I was with everything else in my life, the idea of doing the kind of job I was doing for the rest of my life really brought me down.

One night I was hanging out with a good friend, and as we both talked about how our jobs were not right for us, he recommended that I read Rich Dad, Poor Dad. He said it was an eye opener for him and that I would get a lot out of it. Now, mind you, I hated reading books. The last time I had read a book was in college, four years earlier. He let me borrow the book and that was the beginning of something new for my girlfriend and I.

After finishing the book, my entire outlook on life changed. It was almost like I was reborn! My girlfriend, Monica, after seeing the impact it had on me, decided to read it herself. Amazingly and thankfully, it impacted her just as much. The fact that I now knew what I wanted out of life and that she was on board with me made it that much clearer that I needed to change something. Shortly, we starting going to real estate networking events in the New York/New Jersey area. We bought more Kiyosaki books and even purchased his coaching programming to further help us in our involvement with real estate. One night, as I was browsing the Internet looking for the next event to attend, I came across the RichDadNYC site. I immediately fell in love and had to attend. Monica and I went to a meeting and we left ecstatic. We had found a group with like-minded individuals, run by a great leader with experience in real estate and business who shared everything with his group completely free of charge! Things that we would normally have to pay significant amounts of money to hear were at our very disposal once a month at no cost. We have been attending for over 6 years now and haven't looked back.

The changes since joining the club have been pretty dramatic for us. We have purchased two single-family homes, a duplex, and a 6 unit commercial building in Pennsylvania. We are looking to grow even further within the next upcoming year and purchase several more commercial buildings. We were finally able to take our passion for real estate and turn it into reality! The tools Duane

Harden has given us made it so much easier for us. His guidance and this group have made our dreams accessible. Any challenges we had, Duane was just an e-mail away from answering our questions. Even more rewarding than us climbing our own ladder of success is to see our fellow group mates climb their own ladders and do the things that they are really passionate about. It's an amazing feeling to sort of grow up with a group of people that just 5 years ago were all strangers to us.

We have not been able to resign from our current jobs because in the midst of purchasing our properties, we moved in together and married. As a result, we couldn't go at the pace we originally wanted to as far as purchasing more real estate deals. However, now that all of that is behind us and we are re-focused, the possibilities are endless. Monica is looking to start a business around another passion of hers, travel. She is hoping that she will be able to build this business from the ground up, resign from her current job and continue to grow. I will be purchasing another commercial property within the next several months.

For anyone who is looking to venture into their own business, I would recommend embracing it, however, with caution! Do research online, go to many different networking meetings and establish a team of experts in the field of your choice. You and you alone will never be the "jack of all trades." The faster you realize that, the faster you can go. One major motto we use in our RichDadNYC group is "Your network is your net worth", and this has served us well along our path to financial freedom.

Testimonial 5: More than a Conqueror

As an enlisted soldier in the US Army, I was trained to handle any situation, to see each challenge as a road with obstacles, to identify the obstacles, control for the unknown, and finally plan and execute a series of small steps that would systematically get me and my team to our goal. This training and the use of it allowed me to accomplish things I never dreamed of, personally and academically, but not financially. In the seven years since leaving the service, I had acquired my first college degree, graduating with highest honors, and my second degree from Columbia University, graduating with honors; yet six months after leaving academia, I burned out physically, emotionally and mentally from working three jobs in order to pay for an unsustainable lifestyle.

As a child growing up in a home with a single mother, we lived paycheck to paycheck and I was never taught a single lesson about personal finance. Mass media and peer's habits pointed me towards insatiable consumption and working harder and harder in order to keep up with the Joneses. Graduating from Columbia University in 2010, at one of the lowest points in the economic recession, I worked at a company on Wall Street to pay for my student loans and utility bills; I worked as a barback to pay for my lifestyle, clothes and rent; and I worked as a freelance marketing consultant to pay for my other living expenses. After six months of working six and a half days a week and sleeping five hours nights, I burned out.

The way I was living and the time I spent working was untenable. At that point, a friend of mine who was already a member of the Rich Dad Cash flow group took pity on me and brought me along with him. Meeting Duane and joining the group not only educated me about personal finance, but also allowed me to see through public misinformation and myths about financial planning. Duane and the group taught me not only how to tease out the differences between true assets and liabilities, but more importantly that it's not what's on the balance sheet that matters, but the cash flow generated by the balance sheet.

Since joining the group, I had shed enough liabilities to be able to free myself financially, purchase my own home, generate cash flow from that home, quit all of my jobs, start a career in a position and firm that I love and start my own company. In my entire life, I had never thought of a career in financial services and never had any desire to work within that industry. One year after I joined the Rich Dad group and met Duane, I could not think of anything more fulfilling than to do for others what Duane had done for me. I am currently learning, notice I didn't say working, as a Financial Planner at a firm and I have never been happier.

Concurrent with my new career, and in keeping with the philosophy taught to me by Duane and the cash flow group, I started a tea company with two of my friends. We all grew up in New York during the bubble tea and food truck craze and thought it would be a great idea if we could combine the two. In a city where new bubble tea shops pop up and disappear overnight, I wondered why the turnover rate was so extreme. My partners and I did a lot of research and drank… a lot of tea. We found that most tea shops, like other industries out there, lacked quality control. After conducting quite a bit of research and having no idea how to serve quality tea in the one minute a New Yorker would be willing to wait on the sidewalk for anything, we were left scratching our heads.

Thankfully, a friend of mine from over a decade ago had already established his bubble tea truck in California and it was a huge success. He had invented a process that could control for quality and deliver this delicious product on a large scale, preparing the tea in two minutes flat with capacity for selling 500 cups in one sitting. Needless to say, my partners and I contacted this old friend and we are now are trying to replicate his process in NY. For me, this initiative has two key aspects. First of all, to experience the process of starting my own business so that I can identify with the challenges my clients face and to help them overcome those challenges. Secondly, to turn my childhood passion of bubble tea into my second business.

Although my partners and I know we have a hugely successful product and we had gone through every step as directed by the NYC Department of Commerce to launch our business, we had been thrown so many roadblocks that at several points, I had no idea if we would be able to proceed. I felt so beat down that I didn't know if my tea business was going to fail before it even started. However, the benefits of having a great team, mentor, and the determination to educate yourself is that you will find there is always a way to overcome the hurdles that are placed in front of you. Sometimes you can get around a hurdle and find yourself back on the same path, closer to your goal and sometimes you get around an obstacle to find yourself on a completely different but equally fruitful path. No matter what the outcome of my latest endeavor, it has already been a profitable learning experience.

Testimonial 6: Survive With Nothing

I had always been interested in entrepreneurship & business ownership, but for a long time I had no idea of how to go about pursuing such endeavors. I stumbled upon the cash flow group one Saturday in 2006 and it was the best chance encounter I ever had. There, through the mentorship of Duane, I learned what financial freedom was and how to go about pursuing my ambitions & passions. This has given me the ability to see the world from the vantage point of wealth building and the pursuit of financial freedom. I now see how each decision you make and the events taking place in the world impact this pursuit and my ability to provide for my community, my family and myself.

I'm passionate about the idea of being my own boss, the idea that my success hinges on my own ability to foster ideas, galvanize resources, develop & implement strategies and ultimately bring it all together in such a way that the result is truly awesome.

As a young and aspiring entrepreneur, I had an inherent lack of knowledge. I also had a tendency to over-analyze situations and not be action-oriented. I am grateful and fortunate, as I was able to learn how to overcome these challenges through my involvement in the cashflow group.

In this process, one PIG I identified was franchise ownership. I was able to bring a group of other aspiring business owners together. We pooled financial resources, applied our collective knowledge and invested in an opportunity. We've been in business 2 years now, have seen significant growth over that period and are in the process of acquiring a second franchise unit with plans to develop more opportunities in the near future. We love the basket and bouquet industry and this franchise was the perfect match for us to invest and build our business in.

Throughout the process, my biggest fear to overcome was failure. I've since learned to turn that fear of failure from something that cripples you and prevents you from taking action to something that liberates you and motivates you to achieve your goals and objectives.

My strategy is to find people who are successfully doing what I want to do and learn from them. The reason I decided to pursue franchising is because I saw Duane do it and I thought I could do it too. I came to his group with visions of what I thought I could accomplish, and Duane taught me how to make those visions reality.

I resigned from my corporate job long before I knew what I was going to do with myself. Before I left my job, my financial situation was great. I had more money than I could spend, at least for a young person with no responsibilities in the word. But I didn't like my position in life. I felt like something was off and yearned for more. After I left my job to pursue entrepreneurship, my financial position turned sour. Funds dried up, my credit went into the pits, and it was the best thing that ever happened to me. I learned to survive with nothing. I learned to build a business from the ground up. I'm happy to say my financial situation is slowly beginning to move in the right direction thanks to what I've been able to learn and apply these last few years.

For all those thinking of starting their own business, in spite of the difficulties, my only piece of advice would be to "Go for it!"

Appendix B

Life Assignments

Life Assignment 1: Crab List

Vision: Complete the list below of people you talk to on a regular basis. On the "Good Crab" column list those people who "increase" your life and on the "Bad Crab" column list those people who "decrease" your life. Being able to identify the personality traits of the people around you will help you control the impact of their comments.

<u>Bad Crab</u>   <u>Good Crab</u>

1.   1.

2.   2.

3.   3.

4.   4.

5.   5.

6.   6.

7.   7.

Life Assignment 2: Discovering the Real You

Vision: Great exercise to help you discover who you really are in the investing world.

Part 1: Who You Were?
I want you to dust those cobwebs off and think back who you were 10 years ago and answer the following questions:

Ia) Where did you live?
  a. Address _____
  b. Owned (   ) or Rented (   )
  c. How much was your monthly payment? $ _____

Ib) Where did you work?
  a. Company: _____
  b. Position: _____
  c. Annual Salary: $ _____

Part II: Who Are You Now?
Answer these questions as you exist right now in this moment.

IIa) Where do you live?
  a. Address _____
  b. Own (   ) or Rent (   )
  c. How much is your monthly payment? $_____

IIb) Where do you work?
  a. Company: _____
  b. Position: _____
  c. Annual Salary: $ _____

Part III: Who WIll You Be?
I want you to look ahead the next 5 years and try to envision who you will be and answer the same questions:

IIIa) Where are you living?
  a. Address _____
  b. Own (   ) or Rent (   )
  c. How much is your monthly payment? $_____

IIIb) Where are you working?
  a. Company: _____
  b. Position: _____
  c. Annual Salary: $ _____

Life Assignment 3: Financial Statements

Finding Your "I" in Passion Financial Statements

It is very important to know where you are today. These statements will be the basis for your financial plan. You can set goals and continuously monitor your financial growth. Please click on each worksheet tab and complete your:

1. **Income Statement**—Shows your CashFlow as it is today.

2. **Balance Sheet**—Shows your Net Worth and leveraging power of your current assets to purchase more assets.

3. **Cost of Capital**—Very important and often overlooked. It shows how much you are being charged for your debt. This is always a great starting point in reorganizing this debt to increase your monthly CashFlow.

4. **Working Money**—Spotlight on your investments current rates of return.

Insert or delete rows as needed. You may add additional categories as well. Really utilize this tool so you can get an accurate picture of what story the numbers tell you.

Life Assignment 3: Financial Statements
Income Statement

Money Coming In (Income)

		Monthly Average	Annually Total
A. Earned Income			
Job		$ -	$ -
Self-employment		$ -	$ -
	Subtotal	$ -	$ -
B. Passive Income			
Real Estate (NET)		$ -	$ -
Business (NET)		$ -	$ -
	Subtotal	$ -	$ -
C. Portfolio Income			
Interest		$ -	$ -
Dividends		$ -	$ -
Royalties		$ -	$ -
	Subtotal	$ -	$ -
D. Total Income		$ -	$ -

Money Going Out (Expenses)

		Monthly Average	Annually Total
A. Credit Cards			
1)		$ -	$ -
2)		$ -	$ -
3)		$ -	$ -
4)		$ -	$ -
	Subtotal	$ -	$ -

B. Department Store Cards

1)	$ -	$ -
2)	$ -	$ -
3)	$ -	$ -
4)	$ -	$ -
Subtotal	$ -	$ -

C. School Loans

1)	$ -	$ -
2)	$ -	$ -
Subtotal	$ -	$ -

D. Other Living Expenses

1) Mortgage	$ -	$ -
2) Transportation	$ -	$ -
3) Phone	$ -	$ -
5) Clothing	$ -	$ -
6) Entertainment	$ -	$ -
7) Charity	$ -	$ -
8) Misc.	$ -	$ -
Subtotal	$ -	$ -

E. Total Expenses $ - $ -

Monthly Cash Flow

Passive Income	$ -
Total Monthly Expenses	$ -
Cash Flow	$ -

Reserves

Liquid	0
Liquid + Non-Liquid	0

Life Assignment 3: Financial Statements
Balance Sheet

What You Save (Assets)

Current Balance

A. Liquid Assets

Checking	$ -
Savings	$ -
Subtotal	$ -

B. Investments

IRA/401(k)/403(b)	$ -
Mutual Funds	$ -
Stocks	$ -
Bonds	$ -
Receivables	$ -
Real Estate (Value-Mortgage)	$ -
Business Value (NET)	$ -
Limited Partnerships	$ -
Subtotal	$ -

C. Other Assets

1) Auto	$ -
2)	$ -
3)	$ -
Subtotal	$ -

D. Total Assets | $ -

Money You Spend (Liabilities)

Current Balance

A. Credit Cards

1)	$ -
2)	$ -
Subtotal	$ -

B. Department Store Cards

1)	$ -
2)	$ -
3)	$ -
4)	$ -
Subtotal	$ -

C. School Loans

1)	$ -
2)	$ -
Subtotal	$ -

D. Other Expenses

1) Mortgage	$ -
2) Car Loan Balance	$ -
3) Personal Loans Payable	$ -
4)	$ -
Subtotal	$ -

E. Total Liabilities $ -

What's the Story?

Net Worth

Assets	$ -
Liabilities	$ -
Net Worth	$ -

Life Assignment 3: Financial Statements
<u>Cost of Capital</u>

Creditor Company Name	Current APR	Balance Transfer APR	Monthly Minimum Payment	Current Balance	Credit Line	Available Credit	Last Date Credit Line Increased
	0.00%	0.00%	$ -	$ -	$ -	$ -	
	0.00%	0.00%	$ -	$ -	$ -	$ -	
	0.00%	0.00%	$ -	$ -	$ -	$ -	
	0.00%	0.00%	$ -	$ -	$ -	$ -	
	0.00%	0.00%	$ -	$ -	$ -	$ -	
	0.00%	0.00%	$ -	$ -	$ -	$ -	
	0.00%	0.00%	$ -	$ -	$ -	$ -	
	0.00%	0.00%	$ -	$ -	$ -	$ -	
	0.00%	0.00%	$ -	$ -	$ -	$ -	
	0.00%	0.00%	$ -	$ -	$ -	$ -	
	0.00%	0.00%	$ -	$ -	$ -	$ -	
	0.00%	0.00%	$ -	$ -	$ -	$ -	
Totals	0.00%	0.00%	$ -	$ -	$ -	$ -	

Your revolving balance in relation to your available credit plays an important role in determining your credit score.

Life Assignment 3: Financial Statements
<u>Working Money</u>

Bank/Financial Institution Company Name	Interest Rate	Current Balance	Asset Growth
	0.00%	$ -	$ -
	0.00%	$ -	$ -
	0.00%	$ -	$ -
	0.00%	$ -	$ -
	0.00%	$ -	$ -
	0.00%	$ -	$ -
	0.00%	$ -	$ -
	0.00%	$ -	$ -
	0.00%	$ -	$ -
	0.00%	$ -	$ -
	0.00%	$ -	$ -
	0.00%	$ -	$ -
Totals	0.00%	$ -	$ -

Review the interest rate your being paid on your money saved.
Move it around to accounts paying higher rates.

Life Assignment 4: Home Office Space

Vision: Create a clearly defined clutter free space for your home offices. Here are some useful tips:

1. **Create Your Space**—An organized home office is essential to creating a productive work environment. Whether in your bedroom, living room, kitchen area, or any other living space in your home, make sure the space you do create is totally dedicated as your workspace. Provide adequate space for your computer and other equipment, a place for reference materials, file cabinet, and supplies. Adequate lighting and ventilation is also essential so consider this if you're creating it in your garage. Defining a separate workspace from your living space will keep you organized and focused on your business.

2. **Keep Your Space Clean**—Your office desk is probably where you will spend most of your time in your home office so it's important to keep it clean. Periodically, you should throw away unnecessary documents that are cluttering up your space.

3. **Everything Has Its Place**—Use desk organizers like pen holders, mail organizers, and filing stations to keep everything organized. Organizers like mail inbox and outbox will be very essential to your success.

Life Assignment 5: What makes you tick?

Vision: This exercise will help you to discover what you're truly passionate about in life. Just read and answer the question and write down each activity as it pops in your mind. Don't worry about the happy & conversion column for now you'll fill that in later.

Question: If time and money were not a factor, what would you be doing right now? That means if you had all the time in the world and all the money in the world what are things you'd do that make you happy?

Answers	Factor	Conversion
_____	____	_____
_____	____	_____
_____	____	_____
_____	____	_____
_____	____	_____
_____	____	_____
_____	____	_____
_____	____	_____
_____	____	_____
_____	____	_____
_____	____	_____

Life Assignment 6: Creating Your "I"

Total Living Expenses = $_____$

Current Passive Income = $_____$

Life Assignment 7: Creed

Vision: Your daily reminder of what your focus should be. When you go through your daily activities and work, you should have this in the back of your mind to help you stay focused and on track to financial freedom.

Date: _____

Signature: _____

Life Assignment 9: Resignation Letter

Vision: Set a date sometime in the future that you will resign from your current employer. Write your sincere resignation letter and keep it in a private place in your workspace. Refer to it when you need moments of motivation to get you back on track to financial freedom.

Date: _____

Dear: _____ ,

Respectfully,

Life Assignment 10: Winner's Circle

Winner's Circle

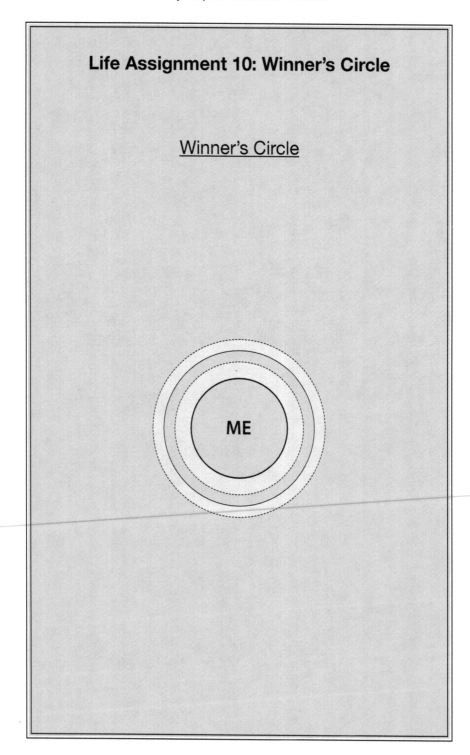

Life Assignment 11: Is It a PIG?

Now that you've decided which business you will create from your "*I*" it's now time to run it through the Rule of 3 Asset Litmus Test. Use your best estimate for the numbers:

Rule #1: Positive Cash Flow—Think about the different income sources that can exist for your business and use them to calculate the income. Think about the fixed cost and variable cost that will exist for your business and use them to calculate your expenses. Use a monthly number.

Income   **Expenses**

Source #1	$_____	Fix #1	$_____	Var #1	+ $_____
Source #2	+ $_____	Fix #2	+ $_____	Var #2	+ $_____
Source #3	+ $_____	Fix #3	+ $_____	Var #3	+ $_____
Source #4	+ $_____	Fix #4	+ $_____	Var #4	+ $_____
Source #5	+ $_____	Total Fix	+ $_____	Total Var	$_____
Total Income	$_____	Total Expenses	$_____		

Monthly Cash Flow = Total Income - Total Expenses

$$= \$\text{_____} \ - \ \$\text{_____}$$
$$= \$\text{_____}$$

Asset Test #1: Does this *PIG* create a positive monthly cash flow?
(   ) Yes or (   ) No

Rule #2: Cash-on-Cash Return on Investment (ROI)—Where are you getting your initial capital from to acquire this investment? If you're using money from your savings, what is the current rate of return on your savings? How much money do you need to take out of your savings? If you are borrowing the money, then put $0 and 0% for Total cash and Cash-on-Cash = ∞ (Infinite)

Total Cash: Investment = $_____   Current Rate of Return = _____ %

Cash-on-Cash ROI = (Monthly Cash Flow *12) / Total Cash Investment

$$= (\$\text{_____} \ *12) \ / \ \$ \text{_____}$$
$$= \$\text{_____} \ / \ \$ \text{_____}$$
$$= \text{_____} \%$$

Asset Test #2: Is the Cash-on-Cash ROI > Current Rate of Return?
(   ) Yes or (   ) No

Rule #3: Appreciation Rate—From what you know of current market conditions, is it "likely" that the value of your asset will increase while you hold it?
(   ) Yes or (   ) No

It's a PIG if you have 3 YES's !!!

Keys To Life

- All you need to **know** . . . is that you will never **know** . . . everything there is to **know** . . . and once you **know** that . . . you can move on!

- Live in the world of abundance and not scarcity!

- Give and it shall be given unto you!

- Whatever you do in life, do it for love and not for money!

- You are what you think and will become what you dream.

- Embrace your fear!!!

- Your network determines your net worth.

- Taking the first leap of faith makes you successful!

Appendix D

Great Resources

- CEOeBooks.com—www.ceoebooks.com—Your resource site to find great books and ebooks for entrepreneurs.

- Kelly Blue Book—www.kbb.com—Find out an approximate value for your car. You will need this information to complete your Financial Statements.

- BankRate.com—www.bankrate.com—You can compare mortgage interest rates from different lenders and find the bank paying the highest interest rate on checking, savings, and CD accounts.

- Mint.com—www.mint.com—My favorite site to help me manage my money. It provides a great snapshot of my net worth. There is a mobile application available for the site as well.

- BillShrink—www.billshrink.com—This site is awesome for analyzing your cell phone bill and making recommendations as to which carrier offers the best plan for your average usage.

- Federal Housing Finance Agency (FHFA)—www.fhfa.gov—The House Price Index (HPI) is a useful tool to help determine the appreciation rate for the area in which your property is located.

- Small Business Administration (SBA)—www.sba.gov—You can find a comprehensive business plan you can complete online. Request an appointment with your local SBA field office for assistance in completing your business plan and finding financing for your business. Use the SBA as your primary resource for your business needs.

- Scotsman Guide—www.scotsmanguide.com—Use this site to help you find private money loans from hard money lenders.

- Internal Revenue Service (IRS)—www.irs.gov—Obtain your Employee Tax Identification Number (EIN) from this site.

- Dun & Bradstreet—www.dnb.com—Register your business on this site. Will be useful in the future for establishing business credit.

- Meetup.com—www.meetup.com—Great site to find local groups for networking.

- AnnualCreditReport.com—www.annualcreditreport.com—Obtain a FREE copy of your credit report.

- GMAIL.com—www.gmail.com—Create a Google email account and Google voice phone number for your business.

- Vistaprint.com—www.vistaprint.com—You can order free business cards from this company.